New Thinking
On
Higher Education

New Thinking
On
Higher Education
Creating a Context for Change

JOEL W. MEYERSON
Editor

Forum for the Future of Higher Education

Series Volume One

ANKER PUBLISHING COMPANY, INC.
Bolton, MA

New Thinking on Higher Education
Creating a Context for Change

ISBN 1-882982-23-1

Composition by Hoyle Ballard & Company
Cover design by Boynton Hue Studio

Anker Publishing Company, Inc.
176 Ballville Road
P.O. Box 249
Bolton, MA 01740-0249 USA

About the Authors

Maureen E. Devlin. Maureen Devlin is director of research and publications for the Forum for the Future of Higher Education. She is also a senior policy analyst for the Massachusetts Board of Higher Education. She was primary author of *Mindpower in Massachusetts: The Commonwealth's Natural Resource,* a report on the condition of public higher education in the state. Prior to her association with the board, she was a higher education consultant with Coopers & Lybrand. Devlin also served as associate staff director of the Knight Foundation Commission on Intercollegiate Athletics, a blue-ribbon panel that produced a reform agenda for college sports in the early 1990s.

Cynthia McPherson Frantz. Cynthia McPherson Frantz is a laboratory instructor in the department of psychology at the University of Massachusetts, Amherst. She has worked as a statistical consultant at UMass, Amherst College, and Ridefilm Corporation. She is coauthor of "The Impact of Trauma on Meaning: From a Meaningless World to Meaningful Life," which appeared as a chapter in *The Transformation of Meaning in Psychological Therapies: Integrating Theory and Practice* (Power & Brewin, 1997).

George R. Goethals. George Goethals is former provost (1990-1995) of Williams College. Working at Williams since 1970, he currently serves as chair of the psychology department. Over the course of his career, he has taken several visiting professorships and research positions at universities throughout the U.S. and Canada, including Princeton University, University of Virginia, University of Waterloo, University of Santa Barbara, and University of Massachusetts, Amherst. He is the author of many publications, including the forthcoming textbook *Adjustment: Pathways to Personal Growth* (with S. Worchel & L. Heatherington, Allyn & Bacon, 1999) and journal article "Subsidy Shock: Reshaping Judgments of College Sticker Prices" (with C. M. Frantz, *Basic and Applied Psychology,* in press).

C. Jackson Grayson, Jr. Jack Grayson is chairman of the American Productivity & Quality Center in Houston, Texas. He has been professor and dean of the Tulane University School of Business Administration and the Southern Methodist University School of Business Administration. He has also been on the business faculty of IMEDE (Switzerland) and INSEAD (France). Under President Nixon, from 1971-1973, Grayson served as chairman of the US Price Commission. He also served on President Carter's Commission on a National Agenda for the 1980s and President Reagan's National Productivity Advisory Committee. He is currently on the board of Browning-Ferris Industries. He is the author of over 60 monographs and articles, including two books: *Confessions of a Price Controller* and *American Business: A Two-Minute Warning.*

Brian L. Hawkins. Brian Hawkins is senior vice president for academic planning and administration at Brown University. Prior to assuming his current position in 1992, he was Brown's vice president for computing and information services. Before coming to Brown, Hawkins served as associate vice president for academic affairs and associate vice president for computing and telecommunications at Drexel University, and as assistant dean of the College of Business and associate professor of management at the University of Texas at San Antonio. Hawkins has served on the board of directors of CAUSE and EDUCOM as well as advising Microsoft, Sun Microsystems, and Apple Computer on higher education issues. He is the author of *Organizing and Managing Information Resources on Campus* and over 40 articles, including "Planning for the National Electronic Library" and "Preparing for the Next Wave of Computing on Campus."

Richard N. Katz. Richard Katz is vice president of EDUCAUSE, the new higher education information technology association formed by the consolidation of Educom and CAUSE. At EDUCAUSE, Katz is responsible for developing and delivering the association's educational program through a variety of international conferences, workshops, seminars and management institutes, as well as for member and corporate relations and outreach, and research and development. Prior to joining the association in 1996, Katz held a variety of management and executive positions over 14 years at the University of California. As executive director of business planning and practices, he was responsible for the design and implementation of many of the nine-campus UC system's strategic management initiatives. Katz is the author, coauthor or editor of more than 20 books, monographs, and articles on a variety of management and technology topics, including *Sustaining Excellence in the 21st Century: A Vision and Strategies for University Administration.*

Michael J. Kelly. Michael Kelly is university vice president and chief operating officer of Georgetown University where he has responsibility for day-to-day management of the university. Prior to coming to Georgetown, he was dean of the University of Maryland School of Law from 1974 to 1991, where he was cofounder of the Coastal and Environmental Policy Program. Kelly has also served as counsel to the mayors of Baltimore and Boston, chairman of the Baltimore Board of Ethics and Housing Authority, and alumni trustee of Princeton University. He is the author of *Lives of Lawyers: Journeys in the Organization of Practice* (University of Michigan Press, 1994) and numerous articles and monographs including "Enhancing the Competence of Lawyers" and "Legal Ethics and Legal Education."

Joel W. Meyerson. Joel Meyerson is director of the Forum for the Future of Higher Education and chairman emeritus of the higher education and nonprofit practices of Coopers & Lybrand. Previously, he codirected the forum's predecessors, the Stanford (University) Forum for Higher Education Futures, and the Forum for College Financing at Columbia University. He has served on several advisory panels, including the Massachusetts Board of Regents task forces on capital maintenance and tuition policy, and has lectured at the Harvard Institute for Educational Management. Meyerson has authored, coauthored, or edited many books, including *Revitalizing Higher Education, International Challenges to American Colleges and Universities, Strategy and Finance in Higher Education, Productivity and Higher Education, Financing Higher Education in a Changing Economy, Alternative Approaches to Tuition Financing,* and *Strategic Analysis: Using Comparative Data to Better Understand Your Institution.*

James S. Roberts. James Roberts is vice provost for budgets and planning at Duke University. At Duke, he is responsible for budget, personnel management, financial planning, and institutional research for academic programs. As a member of the president's ad hoc strategic planning committee, Roberts was the principal author of the university's long-range plan, "Shaping Our Future: A Young University Faces a New Century." He currently serves on the president's advisory committee on resources and the university steering committee on work process design. Prior to assuming his current position, Roberts served as assistant provost for financial affairs, and director of academic budgets and the academic budget office, all at Duke. In addition to his administrative appointment, he is an adjunct professor of history and the author of *Drink, Temperance, and the Working Class in Nineteenth Century Germany.*

Frederick A. Rogers. Frederick Rogers is senior vice president and CFO of Cornell University. Previously he was Cornell's vice president for finance and treasurer. Prior to joining Cornell, Rogers was at Carnegie Mellon University for 16 years, where he was vice president for business affairs and director of planning and administrative systems. He was also executive assistant to the secretary of labor and industry of the Commonwealth of Pennsylvania while on leave from Carnegie Mellon. Rogers has served as chairman of the Financial Management Committee of the National Association of College and University Business Officers (NACUBO) and is on the board of directors of Eastern Association of College and University Business Officers (EACUBO). He has served as director of the Wheeling Pittsburgh Steel Corporation and is a trustee and vice chairman of the board of the Lebanese American University. He is currently on the board of directors of the Council on Government Relations. Rogers is a founder of Cornell's Administrative Management Institute, where he continues to serve as a director.

Marshall W. Van Alstyne. Marshall Van Alstyne is assistant professor at the University of Michigan, where he teaches courses in information economics, electronic commerce, and computer simulation. He joined the faculty at the School of Information in 1997 after working as a technology management consultant and co-founding a high-tech software venture that provided decision support tools to higher education institutions, including the California State University system. Past consulting clients include several Fortune 500 companies and US government agencies. Since 1995, Van Alstyne has published in numerous journals, including *Science, Decision Support Systems, Sloan Management Review,* and the *Journal of Organizational Computing and Electronic Commerce.* His research has also been the subject of radio broadcasts in the U.S. and Canada.

Gordon C. Winston. Gordon Winston is the Orrin Sage Professor of Political Economy and professor of economics at Williams College. He is the codirector of the Williams Project on the Economics of Higher Education. Winston served as provost of Williams College from 1988 to 1990. His current research focuses on the economics of higher education, including collegiate wealth and economic information for governance and the time-specific modeling of production, consumption, work, and exchange. He is the author or coauthor of numerous journal articles and books, including *Paying the Piper: Productivity, Incentives, and Financing in US Higher Education* (with Michael McPherson and Morton Schapiro). At the 1992 Stanford Forum Symposium, Winston presented a paper on "New Dangers in Old Traditions: The Reporting of Economic Performance in Colleges and Universities."

Forum for the Future of Higher Education

The Forum for the Future of Higher Education is a community of academic leaders and scholars from across the country who convene annually to explore new thinking on higher education. The Forum facilitates shared inquiry and collaboration on issues likely to influence the future of higher education—primarily in finance and economics, structure and strategy, and technology and learning. The Forum sponsors research, presents findings at annual symposia, and disseminates information throughout higher education. The Forum was previously resident at Stanford University and was known as the Stanford Forum for Higher Education Futures. Today, the Forum is an independent, nonprofit organization affiliated with Yale University.

The Forum for the Future of Higher Education is made possible through generous support from:

Coopers & Lybrand	First Marblehead Corporation
Goldman Sachs	International Business Machines (IBM)
Morgan Stanley	J. P. Morgan
Lehman Brothers	Prager McCarthy & Sealy

United Educators, Insurance Risk

Support to inform leaders from independent California colleges and universities of new ideas on the future of higher education is provided by The James Irvine Foundation.

Support for research on technology and education is provided by a special grant from IBM.

In addition to other support, Coopers & Lybrand provides structural, logistical, and production support for the Forum. For more information about the Forum, please contact:

Forum for the Future of Higher Education
Yale University
P. O. Box 208304
New Haven, CT 06520-8304

Contents

Introduction

Maureen E. Devlin

Colleges and universities play an integral role in American life. Over 14 million students enroll in nearly 4,000 two- and four-year institutions of higher learning every year. Cultural activities sponsored by these institutions reach even greater numbers of people. Faculty members, in addition to teaching, conduct research, expanding the boundaries of knowledge in every direction and affecting virtually every United States citizen.

During the 1995-96 academic year, students spent nearly $55 billion on tuition expenses for their education. Federal financial aid for higher education exceeded $37 billion, and federal support for university research was approximately $12 billion. The following year, state expenditures for operating expenses exceeded $46 billion.

Clearly, American higher education does not exist in a vacuum. The synergetic relationship between higher education, the nation, states, and its citizens—the world beyond the campus gates—means that colleges and universities are subject to a number of forces, many largely beyond their control. The economy, increased public interest and scrutiny, and technological applications are primary examples of outside influences forcing higher education leaders to adapt and think creatively. Comfortable, business-as-usual practices, or isolationist thinking will not suffice to meet the challenges facing today's higher education leaders.

How should higher education leaders guide their institutions through these times of change and establish a proper course for the next century? Participants in the 1996 symposium of the Forum for the Future of Higher Education considered these questions and presented insights and models for strategic thinking broadly related to the economics of higher education; institutional mission, particularly as it effects positive change and accountability; and technology.

ECONOMICS

Downsizing, reengineering, and total quality management (TQM)—
the buzzwords, if not the processes—are familiar to all higher education leaders struggling to cut costs, increase efficiencies, and do more
with less. These business-like imperatives have achieved a new domi-
nance on campuses, where in the past idealistic goals related to education and knowledge frequently prevailed over economic concerns.
Increasing costs and resultant rising tuitions have changed that land-
scape dramatically, as meanwhile the public and their representatives
have raised an ever-louder outcry over prices.

While higher education institutions are being forced to reenvision
themselves and operate more like businesses, their fundamental nature
as nonprofits limits the usefulness of the business and industry model.
Gordon C. Winston maintains that if higher education is going to
effectively evaluate, predict, and control the sweeping changes affecting it, we must have a clear understanding of the distinct nature of our
institutions. He outlines several major economic characteristics that
make a nonprofit college or university different from a for-profit firm.

The first is a "nondistribution constraint," meaning that while
nonprofits may actually turn a profit, there are by law no owners to
whom to distribute such profits. This may reduce pressures on managers to operate efficiently. Because of the nondistribution constraint,
nonprofits tend to be most useful in what are known as "trust markets," where customers do not necessarily know what they are buying,
such as in education or perhaps nursing homes or daycare. In these situations, customers have more reason to trust a nonprofit. Winston
emphasizes the remarkable extent to which people do not really know
what they are buying when choosing a college or university. Thus, reputation and "animal hunches" loom large in final decisions. It follows,
then, that public trust in higher education is of critical importance.

Second, managers of nonprofits typically have more idealistic
goals than those of normal business firms. These goals affect decision-
making in unbusinesslike ways, such as the provision of need-based
financial aid to provide student opportunity and access.

Third, nonprofits are distinguished by their revenue sources: Colleges and universities sell a product—education—for which they receive tuition, and they receive income from charitable contributions. These donations mean that colleges and universities do not have to charge a price that covers the costs of the education they provide. Instead, depending upon their level of donative revenues, they can subsidize students by charging less tuition than it costs to educate them. Institutions vary dramatically in the extent to which they can subsidize the education they offer; Winston believes that these subsidy differences may be the most fundamental element in the economics of higher education.

Winston's model of the higher education market flows from the notion of subsidies. First, institutions use subsidies to influence the quality of the students they admit, as follows: A high subsidy—making the college a "better deal"—creates excess demand, assuming stable class size. The school chooses the best applicants, building a strong student body that benefits from proven positive peer effects, where students help educate fellow students. A high quality student body, in turn, builds the institution's reputation, a critical factor influencing more and more students to apply for admission, thus increasing selectivity another notch.

Implicit in this feedback loop of student quality on student demand is the public consensus that student quality is a direct signal of college quality. It all starts with differences in the school's wealth—its access to donative resources with which it can subsidize the education it offers.

The higher education market is a hierarchy, with institutions sorted by the size of their endowments, appropriations, and gifts. These resources, which support institutions' ability to provide subsidies, compound their advantage by the effects of student quality feedback. Higher education has been identified as a classic "winner-take-all" market.

The nature of the higher education market has two key effects. The first is how schools organize themselves to take advantage of student quality, or compensate for its absence. Schools of less student quality are markedly less residential, more dependent upon distance learning, and offer more vocational degree and adult education programs. Part-time programs also are more common. Each of these characteristics deemphasizes the role of the student body in the education offered.

The second key effect clearly illustrates differences between a non-profit institution and a business. Higher education is facing increased enrollments estimated at 10% to 30% over the next decade. That sort of increase in demand would be great news in any for-profit industry, whereas, instead, it has generated genuine panic in higher education. The more students that must be educated, the greater the level of subsidies institutions must provide. In this respect, there are no economies of scale. Institutions have fixed resources (endowments, physical plant, etc.), not fixed costs, that would have to be spread out over more students, reducing the subsidy each receives. A lower subsidy implies less demand, then less selectivity, lower student quality, and lower educational quality.

Private schools, understandably, have been reluctant to expand. Public schools, too, may behave increasingly like privates as their funding bases gradually shift from appropriations tied to enrollments toward block grants, and as they accumulate more endowment wealth.

Winston emphasizes the importance of legislators, donors, trustees, and administrators understanding the higher education market—and the limits of conventional economic analyses and intuition—when addressing the economic challenges that lie ahead for higher education.

Winston's model is based upon the assumption of public knowledge and understanding of the value of subsidies offered by colleges and universities and the effect such knowledge has on demand. Cynthia McPherson Frantz and George R. Goethals tested the validity of this assumption as part of a study they conducted to test the hypotheses that: 1) people think college tuitions are too high; 2) people know very little about the extent to which colleges and universities subsidize their students; and 3) providing people with subsidy information leads them to judge the prices that such schools charge as more reasonable.

Frantz and Goethals surveyed public and private college and university students and K-12 teachers. Their results offer strong, but qualified support for all three hypotheses. First, people generally thought public institutions charges were reasonable but tended to think that private institutions were unreasonable. Second, people generally were aware of subsidies provided by public institutions but in many cases were unaware of the subsidies provided by private colleges and universities. Third, after receiving subsidy information, people increased their reasonableness ratings of private school tuitions but not those of public schools.

In light of Winston's model, the key question may be whether private school students were aware of the extent of subsidies at private institutions, and whether they thought tuition at privates was reasonable. Such, in fact, was the case: Private school students' estimates of the total costs of providing higher education were more accurate than public school students, who evidently thought that private schools make a large profit on each student. Further, private school students consistently gave private school (and public's) tuition levels higher reasonableness ratings than did public school students.

However, Frantz and Goethals' work implies a widespread lack of knowledge of subsidies. Considering that such knowledge is fundamental to creating and maintaining the demand-selectivity-quality loop described by Winston, efforts to increase awareness of subsidies could benefit institutions, particularly those whose subsidies and tuitions are high but which may not be well known or have particularly strong reputations.

In Winston's "winner-take-all" scenario, there would appear to be little room at the top for many selective, expensive private colleges and universities. James S. Roberts assesses the strength of that market by analyzing the position of Duke University.

Duke is a strong player in the high cost/high value segment of American higher education. As such, its success depends very much on its ability to invest substantially more in the education of each student than it charges for tuition—that is, to subsidize students and create excess demand. Roberts notes that as tuition differentiation among leading institutions diminishes, the strength of endowment support for academic programs will be crucial for success. Duke must be able to compete with its peers for the best faculty and maintain and upgrade its facilities, particularly in the technological realm.

Further, a genuine commitment to need-blind admissions and the ability to meet full need are essential to allowing institutions to choose a student body of quality and breadth without regard to ability to pay. Roberts sees this freedom to select the best students as a key ingredient in enhancing educational quality and sustaining market position. It also may be the best answer to those concerned about "sticker shock" over today's college costs.

Because of sticker shock and public doubts about performance and effectiveness, cries for greater accountability have escalated to the point where they must be addressed. Roberts outlines an approach to these concerns by highlighting four principal areas in which tools and concepts from business can help demonstrate accountability: 1) increasing administrative efficiency; 2) concentrating resources in areas of greatest comparative advantage; 3) strengthening "customer focus"; and 4) focusing on "value added" activities.

Roberts concludes that while Duke and others have been forced to respond to harsh criticism by adapting and demonstrating accountability on many fronts, student demand for highly selective private institutions will remain strong. High demand in the market place for top tier graduates, translating into higher career wages, is widely recognized. Further, many aspiring students are from families that also have a general understanding of the extent to which higher education is subsidized: They realize that expensive private colleges and universities are a good deal. Roberts also cites Gallup Poll data indicating that public confidence in private higher education is high. In keeping with the Winston model, such confidence is key to success.

MISSION, ACCOUNTABILITY, AND CHANGE

To enable institutions to respond to criticism and economic imperatives to change, Michael J. Kelly proposes a metaphor, or framework, for thinking about fundamental ideas that precipitate change. He suggests a sort of institutional biography, an exercise that serves to sharpen focus on the fundamental characteristics and values of an institution, and provides a larger context through which to view change. By this means, institutions can transform their operations by adopting new and innovative approaches to problem-solving.

Change, Kelly argues, must be viewed in the context of the institution's mission and sense of direction as a whole. An institution will benefit from envisioning its future in specific terms, thus stimulating a vision as to how to get there. Along the way, an institution also should assess its sense of "wholeness." Are tensions on campus normal, and are feelings of comraderie strong enough to build institutional integrity?

Kelly notes that institutions needn't actually write a biography; however, the concept is quite useful as a planning exercise to generate clear thinking about effective and desirable strategies for change. Ultimately, a thoughtful and complete biography serves to identify and project institutional mission, values, traditions, style, and politics into an enabling vision for innovation and change.

Fred Rogers describes in detail Cornell's Project 2000, an effort to transform campus administrative support services. He notes that many comprehensive universities offer abundant opportunity for significantly improved management practices: In the name of autonomy and decentralization, they have allowed duplicate and arcane practices to abound.

In seeking to reengineer its major administrative support systems, Cornell plans to glean best management practices from business, but meanwhile will emphasize its mission and character as a university. In this regard, Cornell is recognizing the differences between the business realm and its own endeavors.

Echoing Kelly's approach, Rogers emphasizes the importance of starting with creation of a vision, largely based on imagining what Cornell would be like in the future. He stresses the power of a succinctly stated, shared vision that enjoys unqualified support from the institution's top leadership. The vision should be repeated at every opportunity to maintain focus, and to remind those affected by reengineering of the ultimate purpose of the changes being wrought. Further, people must be empowered to act on the vision.

Rogers shares several lessons learned from issues arising early in the course of the project. Their first mistake lay in the project structure, consisting of ten committees. Managers of the ten project teams met weekly, but were unsure of who was in charge. Sufficient accountability and authority did not exist. This eventually was resolved by hiring an outside, senior project director.

Further, while the overall project mission and vision were well articulated, confusion remained as to what the project's specific objectives were. Once objectives were clearly defined, the project gained a clearer focus, one much needed to win broad support for achieving objectives. The project evolved from a solely technology-centered effort to a broader initiative to change structure, organization, people, processes, and, finally, technology.

Rogers urges other institutions to undertake similar projects, and not to be discouraged by the enormity of the effort. He acknowledges that not everything can be done perfectly from the beginning, but that a willingness to constantly evaluate and adapt would keep the project on the right path. Along the way, too, achievable, short-term results should be built in for continued motivation. Finally, perhaps most important, Rogers emphasizes the need for campus colleagues to trust and support each other to ultimately achieve success.

Cornell felt compelled to undertake massive change in order to maintain academic excellence. The institution's leadership realized that costs had to be reduced in order to move the university forward on its academic priorities. Their choice was to improve or deteriorate.

Most higher education institutions similarly are being driven toward significant change, either from within or by outside criticism calling for increased accountability and administrative efficiency. Richard N. Katz describes a prevalent institutional response to change, a compliance-based performance architecture in which performance is judged based on rules compliance. This focus tends to confuse procedural compliance with good management and good results. Disproportionate campus administrative effort is directed at compliance with an ever-growing body of rules, where new rules rarely replace old rules.

Katz advocates a new performance architecture based on measures. Despite higher education's reluctance to be measured, he maintains that intelligent measures can help diagnose the health and vitality of an institution, assist in planning, and help form valid assumptions about the future. Katz describes the University of California's efforts to implement a performance measurement system and shares several lessons learned "in the trenches."

First, all measures demand a context. They must be related to a specific goal and be descriptive enough to be meaningful and acceptable to diverse constituencies. The most effective measurement context is that of institutional vision and goals. Therefore, a performance measurement system must begin with and be rooted in institutional mission and vision statements. It must be of a multidimensional nature so as to communicate the complex trade-offs intrinsic to higher education in ways that traditional financial metrics alone cannot do.

Measures should be limited to a critical few, including just those areas of activity for which successful performance ensures the success of the enterprise (at any level) or for which failure puts the enterprise at risk. Concentration on the critical few makes performance measurement less onerous and, most important, focuses attention of those things that are actionable and, ideally, motivate action.

Practically speaking, the cost of obtaining information and data should be balanced with the value of the information obtained. The process of data collection can readily spiral downward into an endless definitional debate. To move forward, it is important to focus on methodological consistency rather than infinitesimal accuracy. Katz's conclusion, consistent with Kelly's and Rogers' themes, is to reemphasize the need to link measures with institutional vision and goals and to situate information within a story of the institution's issues, aspirations, successes, failures, and risks.

Once institutions agree upon measures, the next step is to establish benchmarks or standards of achievement for each measure. Benchmarks often are based on national norms, peer institutions' averages, baseline data, or some other judgment of what ought to be accomplished.

When benchmarks are established based on best practices and the results those generate for institutions, benchmarking is taking place. C. Jackson Grayson describes benchmarking as a powerful restructuring methodology for institutions undergoing change today. It focuses not just on outcomes, but on processes as well.

Grayson outlines a systematic and disciplined benchmarking process to achieve maximum results. First, key processes for benchmarking should be selected based on their centrality to achieving the vision, mission, and goals of the institution. In this regard, his approach to implementing change is consistent with that of Kelly, Rogers, and Katz. Grayson warns that it is tempting to choose processes that are perhaps interesting and easy to affect, but that are not critical to achieving the institutional mission.

Next, an institution should analyze its current processes and their outcomes, and then identify others who are accomplishing the same tasks or processes better or best. He urges colleges and universities to look beyond peers, and beyond higher education, for models, that is, to go "outside the box" in finding best practices.

Finally, institutions should learn all they can about those exemplary processes. To effectively accomplish benchmarking, Grayson says, "action learning"—personal involvement, observation, participation, and site visits—must occur. Once institutions gain this knowledge, they must adapt best practices to their own organizations. Implementation without such customization can diminish results.

Grayson recognizes the reluctance of higher education to embrace the business concept of benchmarking. The customer focus at the heart of benchmarking, for example, has been foreign to many in higher education. Grayson maintains, however, that benchmarking can bring major benefits to higher education, including improvements in quality, productivity, outcomes, student satisfaction, and reduced costs. He also believes that benchmarking can help improve teaching and learning processes as well as administrative processes. To consign benchmarking to the "business" side of the institution, he says, would be to forgo major gains achievable for the heart of the enterprise.

TECHNOLOGY

Marshall Van Alstyne speaks of the challenge to higher education posed by dramatic changes in information technology. To guide strategic thinking as to how to respond to such challenges, he applies a model of the university as an information processor. He describes universities as delivery systems that create, teach, cache, and accredit information. A growing challenge today is that universities charge for information that can be obtained elsewhere at negligible cost to the source.

Information is unique in that its giver still keeps the gift. This nonrivalry nature has led to exponential growth in the amount of information available. Knowledge is one of the few assets that grows most when shared. University processes can very much affect the distribution and sharing of information that drives its growth.

Another key characteristic of information is, in economic terms, the positive externalities it exhibits. That is, when ideas spill into the marketplace, they create shared collective benefits beyond those for the buyer, who thus pays all the costs for a fraction of the benefits. The opposite, negative externalities, are exhibited by goods that pollute, for example. Neither the buyer nor the seller bear the full costs of the good, and so it tends to be overconsumed. On the other hand, goods with positive externalities, such as universities, tend to be underconsumed, undervalued, and underinvested. This makes them primary candidates for government support.

To generate continued support, universities must position themselves as valuable and essential resources in the information age. They must improve their capacity for handling complex information. Van Alstyne recommends a "network organization," which can cope with rising complexity and rapidly changing information. Network organizations are collections of specialized organizations or units that share a common purpose and exercise joint control. Members have distinctive competencies that complement, rather than compete, with one another. Members specialize in areas of comparative advantage, and leave other areas to those best suited to excel in them.

The trick to a successful network environment is to partner for complementary skills. Partners help share risk, provide diverse information input, and distribute decision authority in ways that can increase joint viability. Network organizations also exhibit the flexibility necessary to cope with constant change, a defining characteristic of the information age.

The issue, then, for universities is to determine where best to focus in order to emphasize areas of comparative strength. Which departments or clusters of departments will provide the greatest value? Too little specialization leaves a school with too little to offer to a network organization. Too much specialization, however, leaves one with few occasions to contribute. Once again, a clear understanding and focus on the institution's core mission, vision, and goals will help guide these key strategic decisions.

Of all the areas on campus affected by the information explosion, perhaps none is more subject to change than the library, traditionally the centerpiece of the classic university in its role as the primary repository of information and knowledge. Brian L. Hawkins outlines the scope of change. Due to rising costs and reduced budgets, library buying power has declined 50% since 1990. Factoring in the information explosion, by 2001 libraries will be able to collect only 2% of the share of available information they were archiving 20 years ago. Hawkins also cites the belief of many experts that information is doubling at the incredible rate of every two to three years.

In this environment, the traditional library cannot sustain itself. Historically, the size of an institution's library—the number of volumes it contains—has been an important competitive factor in assessing institutional quality. Scores of institutions duplicate efforts, a particularly disturbing notion when one takes into consideration the conventional wisdom that only 10% of any collection is heavily used, while 90% of the collection is used infrequently, and the vast majority of the collection never circulates.

Hawkins warns that a new paradigm that meets the economic constraints of our institutions, and yet still supports the traditional values of libraries and scholarship, must be developed. Cooperative, electronic storage is crucial. Information should be stored in many formats in locations throughout the world, and be organized, collected, and shared via a central networked organization. The new defining characteristic of quality in a library should evolve from ownership to information access. This model suggests tremendous economies of scale as information is purchased as needed, rather than with the notion that someday someone may have use for it.

The single most essential change necessary to achieve the library of the future is a fundamental change in the way rights are given to publishers for the academic information generated within the higher education community. Professional organizations and other nonprofits can become their own publishers and distribute their materials electronically over the network. Free dissemination of information will begin to address the massive problems raised by giving rights to publishers.

The library of the future envisioned by Hawkins will be less of a place where information is kept than a portal through which students and faculty pass to access the vast information resources of the world. The structure of the networked organization, Hawkins proposes, would reflect that outlined by Van Alstyne. Its key characteristic would be a shift from historic competition to cooperation under which all may thrive.

CONCLUSION

Higher education is on the threshold of enormous change. How well colleges and universities manage that change and rise to take advantage of the opportunities it presents will determine their long-term viability.

Economic factors and sharpening cries for accountability have ushered in strategies and practices previously associated solely with the for-profit business realm. Provided these strategies are appropriately tailored for application to the nonprofit world of higher education, they offer valuable models through which to effect positive change.

Regardless of what sort of change is contemplated, or which aspect of the institution is targeted, a mission-centered approach is fundamental to ultimate success of the endeavor. A clear institutional vision, supported by focused mission and goals statements, should be the starting point and guiding force behind any major strategic initiative toward change.

Finally, change will best be achieved through cooperative rather than competitive relationships with other institutions. The synergetic relationship among colleges and universities and between them and the outside world must be recognized and developed. Only then can the forces of change challenging today's leaders be harnessed so as to enhance the future of higher education.

Why Can't a College Be More Like a Firm?

Gordon C. Winston

In *My Fair Lady*, Rex Harrison asks plaintively, "Why can't a woman be more like a man?" If she were, he thought, she'd be a whole lot easier to understand and to live with. In academic board rooms and state and federal legislative chambers, the question is "Why can't a college be more like a firm?" If it were, so goes the hope, it would be a whole lot easier to understand and to live with.

Some answers are becoming clear: why colleges and universities are, in some very basic ways, inescapably different from business firms. Like men and women, there are a number of important similarities. But like men and women, we can get into a whole lot of trouble if we're not clear about both the similarities and the differences.

There's some urgency to this question because the changes sweeping over higher education are going to be very hard to evaluate and harder to predict and control if we aren't clear about how to understand these institutions and this "industry." In his 1994 Nobel lecture, Doug North described the importance of the "shared mental models" we use to make sense out of the world because they go far to determine what we see and what we don't see and what we make of it all. An inaccurate mental model of higher education disserves us all. If we think colleges are just like firms when they're importantly different from firms, we will make a hash of it.

But colleges and universities do sell goods and services, like education, for a price, like tuition; and they make those goods and services

1

with purchased inputs and hired workers, like fuel oil and professors; and they use a lot of plant and equipment, like classrooms and labs and parks and computers; and they compete hard for customers and for faculty inputs.

So if it walks like a firm and it talks like a firm, isn't it a firm? The answer, pretty clearly, is no. Or, not in a very simple way.

There are half a dozen economic characteristics that make colleges and universities different—fundamentally, economically different— from the for-profit business firms that shape economists' theories and trustees' and legislators' intuitions. Three are due to Henry Hansmann, a Yale Law professor and economist, and concern nonprofit firms in general; three are specific to colleges and universities.

Hansmann described the defining characteristic of nonprofit firms—both legally and economically—as what he called a nondistribution constraint. Nonprofit firms can make profits, but they can't distribute those profits to their owners—their stockholders—and, indeed, they don't have any owners.

One concomitant of this constraint is that nonprofit firms are most useful and most often found in markets where there's asymmetric information, where customers don't really know what they're buying (or often whether they've bought anything at all), like CARE packages for Zaire or, often, daycare or nursing home services. These are "trust markets."

Another concomitant—widely and critically noted—is that there's reduced pressure on management to operate efficiently. With no profits to distribute, neither stockholders nor corporate raiders can put a fear of inefficiency into nonprofit managers.

If the local Ford dealer had to operate under a nondistribution constraint, you'd know that he wasn't earning any personal profit from servicing your car, and you'd therefore have more reason to trust him when he said you needed a brake job; but he might be more likely to do sloppy work.

That goes to Hansmann's second key characteristic: While conceding their imperfection, he described the managers of nonprofit firms as being motivated by different and typically more idealistic goals than the managers of normal business firms.

This is a useful but messy idea. On the one hand everybody knows that the profit maximization motives we attribute to businessmen are an oversimplification—that business people are sometimes motivated by complicated idealistic ends, too. On the other hand, Estelle James argued persuasively some 20 years ago that managers of nonprofits often corrupt the idealistic aims of their organizations to slide profits over from the activities that earn them to other activities that the managers like better; so, according to James, they may use profits from undergraduate education to cross-subsidize graduate education or faculty research or a Rose Bowl team.

But still there remains a significant difference in what drives the managers of nonprofits. The managers of colleges and universities are more idealistically motivated; they care about educational excellence, about student opportunity and access, and about diversity. Essentially idealistic motives clearly underlie need-based financial aid, for one concrete and expensive instance (see Bowen & Breneman).

Third, Hansmann identified two different kinds of nonprofits, distinguished by their revenue sources:

- "Donative nonprofits" rely for revenues on charitable donations in service of ideological purposes; churches are donative nonprofits and so is CARE or the local PBS station. Those donors, like the managers, believe in the purposes of these firms so they donate their money to support them.

- "Commercial nonprofits" sell a product for a price. Hospitals and medical insurance and, again, nursing homes are commercial nonprofits.

But then colleges and universities are a mix; they are "donative-commercial nonprofits" in Hansmann's terms. Part of their income comes from sales revenues—tuition and fees—and part of it comes from charitable contributions, past and present—endowment income and gifts and government appropriations.

With these two sources of income, donative-commercial nonprofits don't have to charge a price that covers their production costs. To the extent that they've got donative revenues, they can give their customers a subsidy, by selling them an expensive product at a cheap price. And colleges and universities do just that. In 1991, the average student at the average college in the U.S. paid $3,100 for an education that cost $10,600 to produce. So she got a subsidy of $7,500. And, I think surprisingly, there's little difference, on average, between public and private schools—average subsidies were $7,800 and $7,200, respectively. We're used to government subsidies intended to affect people's choices, but here we have massive private subsidies, too.

If that Ford dealer were acting like the typical college or university, he'd be selling the Taurus that costs him $20,000 to put on the showroom floor for a price of $6,000. Not on a year-end clearance, but all the time. Year after year. He might charge his poor customers a lower price than his full-pay sticker price buyers, but on average he'd get $6,000 for the $20,000 car. He'd be able to do it, of course—and keep on doing it—because someone cared enough about what he's doing to be willing donate the other $14,000 per car: a private donor or state legislature. The end result is that the selling price is less than production costs, in clear violation of the laws of Economics 101.

Fourth, to a remarkable extent, people simply don't really know what they're buying. And they can't find out until long after the fact. The idea that higher education represents "an investment in human capital" is more significant than is often realized since investment decisions—even for the hard-headed businessman building a factory—are inherently freighted with uncertainty; indeed, with "unknowability." Keynes threw in the towel, saying that investment behavior was dominated by "animal spirits." For an investment in higher education, the outcome can't be known for 20 to 30 years, if then, and, if that weren't problem enough, it's a once-in-a-lifetime decision that can't be corrected next time around ("I went to Harvard the first time, but frankly it wasn't worth it, so I'll get my next undergraduate education at University of Montana"), and it's a decision that people often make protectively on behalf of their beloved children. So the "perfectly informed customer" of economic theory is nowhere to be seen. Buying a college education is more like buying a cancer cure than a car or a house. There's a strong tendency to avoid regret and play it safe and buy what everyone considers "the best" if you can afford it—reputation and animal hunches loom large in the final decision.

The fifth characteristic involves the way it's produced: Higher education is made by a very strange technology, what I've called a "customer-input technology." Colleges and universities can buy one important input to their production only from their own customers; students help educate students. Good fellow-students, other things being equal, will lead to a better education than poor fellow-students. These are the "peer effects" that show up regularly in empirical studies of college quality, and they're certainly apparent to those of us who teach.

This production technology is really very unusual. Think of the Ford dealer, again. It's as if the Taurus you bought would become a better car—the steering would become more responsive and it would need fewer repairs and hold the road better—if the other people buying Tauruses were better drivers. If they were very good, you'd wind up with a Lexus or Mercedes.

So because it affects the quality of the product they make, colleges and universities care about who they sell their product to. Since students differ in their ability to provide this input—to contribute to the education of their fellow students—a good college wants to sell only to good students, those who will do it well. While fierce selection at the top colleges makes the news stories, even the least selective institutions look hard at student quality and exclude the poorest fitting. This is not the anonymous, indifferent market of economic theory, but using it, Rothschild and White showed that when schools simultaneously buy from and sell to their students, it's at a net price that reflects both of those transactions.

The last economic fact on my list has to do with "heterogeneity." Not surprisingly, schools differ very much. And they differ very much in the price they charge for a dollar's worth of their product. So you can buy that Taurus at different prices, or you can buy BMWs and used Geos. A BMW, in fact, will cost you less than a used Geo. It all rests on the fact that some schools are wealthy—depending relatively little on commercial revenues from tuition because they have ample donative revenues from gifts and endowments and physical plant and legislatures—and some schools are poor. So some schools give their students very large subsidies and some give very little. Again, in 1991, the 10% of U.S. schools with the largest student subsidies gave the average student a subsidy worth $21,000 a year; those with the smallest subsidies gave $1,500. I've come to suspect that this—these differences in schools' ability to pay subsidies to their students—is the most fundamental element in the economics of higher education.

Now, let me put these pieces together in a rough model of higher education. It has three parts.

The first piece of the model says that schools use their donative resources—their ability to subsidize students—to influence the quality of the students they get. It works like this:

- A large subsidy means a better bargain for students—they get more for their money: more and better facilities, more distinguished professors, more student services, and so on. Students recognize this. So subsidies influence student demand, and applicants respond to a good deal. And larger subsidies go with higher demand.

- If the school controls its size, student demand translates into excess demand—a queue.

- That queue of would-be customers allows a school to pick and choose; they select students for their qualities in helping to educate other students.

- Because of the difficulty any student faces in knowing what he's buying and what it will do for him, a school's reputation becomes critically important.

- But it all starts with differences in the schools' wealth—their access to nontuition, donative resources. And it ends with a highly differentiated set of colleges whose initially different wealth has turned into differences in student quality. This may, indeed, be the main way that differences in dollar resources translate into differences in college quality; studies like Sarah Turner's show strong institutional SAT effects on returns to education but little or no direct expenditure effects.

- The hierarchy appears, too, to have supported quite different ways of producing higher education, different ways of organizing that use or economize on scarce student quality. Those schools that can command a great deal of student quality organize themselves to take advantage of its abundance, and they amplify its effects by increasing student interaction. They are residential, they have small classes and nonvocational curricula, they're often isolated, etc. Schools with lower student quality organize themselves to get by without it, de-emphasizing student interaction. They have more part-time students who are older, more commuters, and, in the extreme, more of distance learning where student interaction can play little role, if any.

The second piece of the model is a feedback of student quality on student demand and therefore on student quality, and so on, a fact of central importance to admissions offices and *U.S. News.* (Two articles in *Change* and *The Wall Street Journal* described colleges' efforts to fudge the data on their student quality—so important is it to their standing in the market and their ability to sell their product.) So student quality is a direct signal of college quality—"These are the people who'll educate you." There is also an anticipated halo or network effect as one becomes first a student and then an alum, admitted to the networks of that school's graduates "with all the rights, honors, and privileges appertaining thereto" (to borrow from Williams' commencement rhetoric).

The third piece of the model asks what a market of such firms looks like. It's certainly not flat, like the competitive market. It's a hierarchy. But the hierarchy isn't based on size or number of firms or number of customers, as in conventional oligopolies or oligopsonies of economic theory. It's by the size of their donative wealth, the endowments and appropriations and gifts that support their ability to give an educational subsidy and then compound that advantage by the student quality feedback. The rich get richer and the rich have been getting richer for a long time. It's no accident that higher education was the first market Frank and Cook identified as "winner-take-all."

So the higher education market, already separated along regional lines—and sometimes ideological lines among denominational schools—is also highly hierarchical, differentiated by donative wealth into vaguely delineated and overlapping bands that have little competitive interaction. At the top are schools characterized by large subsidies and excess demand and student selectivity; at the bottom are schools characterized by excess supply; in the middle are the schools facing quality/quantity tradeoffs and the unpleasant choices of enrollment management.

There are a whole lot of numbers lying behind all this but maybe they can be summarized in Figures 1-3. They are based on most of the 3,000 or so colleges and universities in the U.S. and the IPEDS data they reported to the government for 1990-91.

Figure 1.1

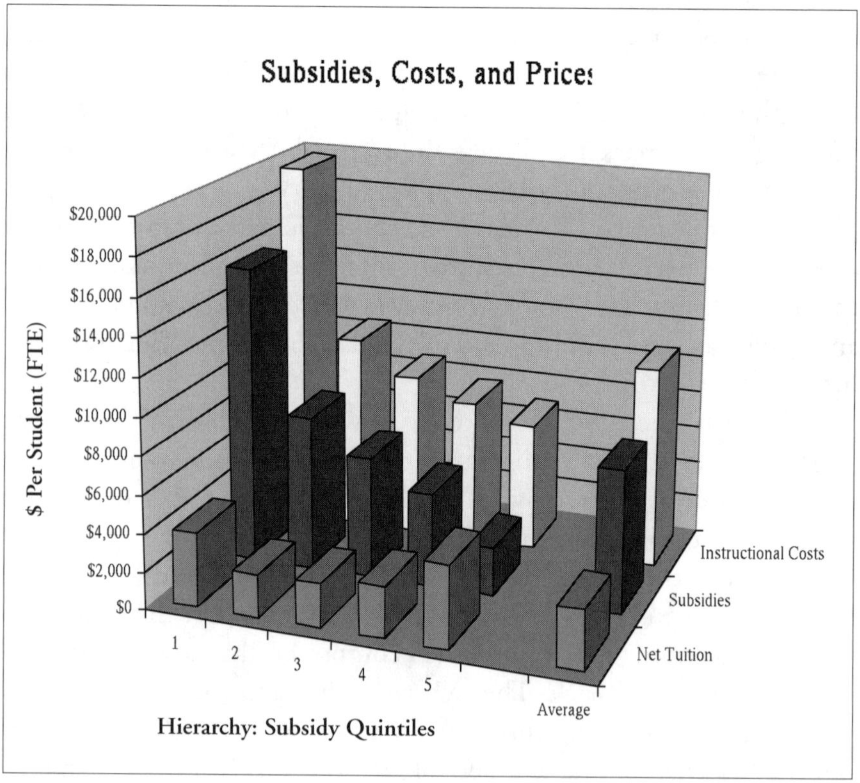

Subsidies, Costs, and Prices

The first figure pictures the average yearly subsidy provided by U.S. colleges and universities, the net price that students actually pay, and the amount spent on their education. (Only two of these are independent; subsidies are measured as educational cost per student minus net price.) The three bars on the far right describe the fact already noted that, on average over all schools, the cost of a year's education is $10,600 for which the student pays $3,100 so he gets a subsidy of $7,500. The bars on the left give the same information but for the hierarchy of schools, ranked by the size of their student subsidies—their wealth—from richest to poorest, left to right. Quintile rankings are pretty crude—deciles tell a better story, especially about the very top winner-take-all schools, but quintiles are easier to read (and all of these relationships within the subsidy hierarchy are very significant, statistically). This figure shows that as subsidies decline, so does spending on a student's education. And so, for a while, does the price the student has to pay for his education. But, surprisingly I think, that net price falls only at the top, then it turns up in the bottom two quintiles. Students at the schools with the smallest subsidies that spend the least on their students' educations make them pay more out of pocket than those further up the hierarchy.

In the next figure, measures of student quality are plotted against the same subsidy hierarchy. Most familiar are schools' average SAT scores (that fall from 1041 in the top quintile to 931 in the bottom) and the share of applicants accepted (that rises from 73% in the top quintile to 86% in the bottom). The graph also shows a decline in the proportion of freshmen coming from the top 10% of their high school class (from 30% at the top to 14% at the bottom). Other measures like the proportion of freshmen who score over 600 on the Math SAT tell the same story but clutter the graph. (All of these relationships are statistically quite significant.)

The last figure pictures some ready indicators of "educational technology" to show how schools arrange themselves to take advantage of student quality, or compensate for its absence. It also includes some measures that would act primarily to increase the demand pool; there is considerable overlap in these. So the colleges with less of student quality are markedly less residential (from 60% of undergraduates in dorms at the top to 36% at the bottom) and more dependent on distance learning (8% of the schools at the top have such programs, 18% at the bottom) and vocational degree programs (7% to

12%). The proportion of schools with adult education programs rises (from 70% at the top to more than 90% in the fourth quintile) before falling back (to 79% in the fifth). Part-time programs also rise to the middle of the ranking and then fall.

Figure 1.2

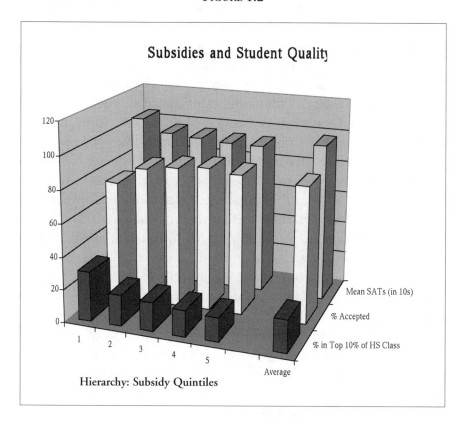

So what? I think the most basic answer to that always-crucial question remains that of understanding. If we aren't clear about how higher education functions, then we will be unlikely to see or predict or evaluate the changes that are overtaking us. There's that useful old saw that we rarely get in trouble because of things we don't know—we get into trouble because of things we think we know, but we don't. We can ill afford to be wrong about the economic structure of higher education, confusing it with a for-profit industry.

FIGURE 1.3

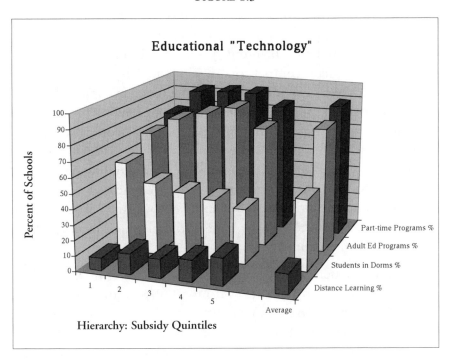

But that's pretty abstract. So let me end with some more concrete illustrations:

■ We're facing an increase in enrollments over the next decade estimated at 10% to 30%. That kind of demand increase would be cause for dancing in the streets in any for-profit industry. But for higher education, it is cause, instead, for genuine panic. If it comes to pass that 3 million more students enter U.S. colleges and universities, they will bring with them (based on our 1991 numbers) an additional $9.3 billion in net tuition revenues, but they will also bring an additional $32 billion in costs if quality is to be maintained at 1991 levels. That will require $22.7 billion of additional nontuition resources. From somewhere. Our for-profit intuition doesn't prepare us for a dilemma like this.

- The "snooties" at the very top of the hierarchy appear to be insulated from market forces. They can give very large subsidies that generate long queues of highly able applicants from whom they select only the best. For-profit firms with all that demand would invite immediate competitors, but in the Alice-in-Wonderland economics of higher education, competitors don't appear because, tradition and reputation aside, they would have to provide their students with huge subsidies to do so. They would have to sell their product for about 25 cents on the dollar of cost and do it, not just to break into the market, but from day-one onward. So are the colleges and universities at the top of the hierarchy impervious to market pressures? Probably not, but that isn't a question that can be answered on the basis of theories and intuitions from the for-profit sector.

- For a firm, increased size often brings economies of scale—fixed costs are spread over more and more output. But for a college that's dependent on endowment and existing physical plant to support its student subsidies—as most private schools are—increased size spreads those fixed resources over more and more students, reducing the average subsidy each one can get. Smaller subsidies, less demand. And if that weren't reason enough to be wary of expansion, increased size reduces selectivity from any given applicant pool. Less selectivity, lower student quality, lower educational quality. So for two good reasons, private schools have long been reluctant to expand. Public schools, in contrast, have usually been supported by "capitation"—appropriations tied to enrollments—to encourage expansion, hence citizen access to higher education. They escape the gloomy arithmetic of a larger denominator that rules the private sector. But that's changing. Capitation is being replaced by fixed block grants to public colleges, as in the California system, and as they accumulate more endowment wealth, public colleges and universities will increasingly have the same incentives the private schools have had to restrict access. More students will come to mean more costs but not more income. So if the trend to block grants continues, it can be anticipated that public institutions will behave increasingly like private ones with access restricted by both size and selectivity.

It may seem paradoxical that these insights into the economic uniqueness of higher education rest solely on economic analysis, on using its ideas and structure to see the limitations of conventional economic analysis and intuition. But, without careful attention to costs and prices and production technologies and, especially to markets— for students and student quality and faculty quality—higher education would remain very hard to understand, and those making economic decisions about higher education (legislators, donors, trustees, administrators) would be hard-pressed to avoid disastrous errors in addressing the challenges that lie ahead.

REFERENCES

Bowen, W. G., & Breneman, D. (1993, Winter). Student aid: Price discount or educational investment? *Brookings Review,* 11, 28-31.

Clotfelter, C. T. (1996b). *Buying the best: Cost escalation in elite higher education.* Princeton, NJ: Princeton University Press.

Cook, P. J., & Frank, R. H. (1993). The growing concentration of top students in elite schools. In C. T. Clotfelter & M. Rothschild (Eds.), *Studies of supply and demand in higher education:* A National Bureau of Economic research project report. Chicago, IL: University of Chicago Press.

Hansmann, H. (1981, November). The rationale for exempting non-profit organizations from corporate income taxation. *Yale Law Journal,* 91, 54-100.

James, E. (1978, Spring). Product mix and cost disaggregation: A reinterpretation of the economics of higher education. *Journal of Human Resources,* 13, 157-86.

Rose-Ackerman, S. (1996, June). Altruism, nonprofits, and economic theory. *Journal of Economic Literature,* 34, 701-728.

Rothschild, M., & White, L. J. (1995, June). The analytics of pricing in higher education and other services in which customers are inputs. *Journal of Political Economy,* 103, 573-86.

Stecklow, S. (1995, April 5). Cheat sheets: Colleges inflate SATs and graduation rates in popular guidebooks. *Wall Street Journal,* p. 1.

Turner, S. (1996). A note on changes in the returns to college quality. Ann Arbor, MI: University of Michigan.

Webster, D. S. (1992, March/April). Rankings of undergraduate education in *U.S. News and World Report* and *Money:* Are they any good? *Change,* pp. 19-31.

Winston, G. C., & Yen, I. (1995, July). *Costs, prices, subsidies, and aid in U.S. Higher Education.* Williamstown, MA: Discussion paper 32, the Williams Project on the Economics of Higher Education.

Winston, G. C. (1996, November). *The economic structure of higher education: Subsidies, customer inputs, and hierarchy.* Williamstown, MA: Discussion paper 40, the Williams Project on the Economics of Higher Education.

Acknowledgements

The Andrew W. Mellon Foundation supported the work that lies behind this paper through its generous support of the Williams Project on the Economics of Higher Education. An early version was presented at the Stanford Forum in Aspen in October 1996 and it came away much improved. It was published in *Change* magazine, September/October, 1997. Comments and encouragement came, too, from Frank Oakley, Hank Payne, Sarah Turner, Larry Litten, Jim Kolesar, Jo Procter, Ethan Lewis, Dave Breneman, Dick Chait, John Chandler, James Shulman, Bill Massy, Joel Meyerson, Morty Schapiro, and Mel Elfin.

2

Thinking Seriously about Paying for College: The Large Effects of a Little Thought

George R. Goethals
Cynthia McPherson Frantz

The high price of attending college has generated a great deal of discussion and some heated controversy in recent years. In 1996, *Newsweek* carried a cover story with a headline proclaiming "$1,000 a week: the scary cost of college" (Morganthau & Nayyar, 1996). A more recent column in *The Boston Globe* pictured a family hunched over a table with a tuition bill and a calculator trying to figure out how to pay the price: "The tuition alone is astronomical. Add in mandatory fees, housing, textbooks, equipment—it's overwhelming. Even if they qualify for financial aid, they're still looking at crushing bills" (Jacoby, 1997). While economists have written thoughtfully about the issue of college affordability, the media have generally fed the popular conception that college prices are unreasonable, unjustified, and unpayable.

In the context of thinking seriously about the ways colleges and universities ought to approach the difficult issue of pricing, it might be helpful to know something about the way students think about the amount they pay, and what they get for their money. Our research suggests that while students tend to think that colleges charge too much, a little information and a little thought often leads them to change their opinions. Their initial judgments about the reasonableness of college charges appear to be negative reflexive reactions based on popular treatments of the price issue, such as those just noted. However, students revise those initial judgments when they've thought a little more about what they're getting for what they're paying.

THE IMPACT OF SUBSIDY INFORMATION

Our first studies asked whether students have much understanding of how much it costs colleges to produce their educations. We suspected that they knew very little, and that being clued in might change their thinking. The facts of the matter are these: Colleges and universities subsidize their students' educations to a high degree, especially when the costs of the services provided by land, buildings, and equipment are considered (Winston & Yen, 1995). The subsidies, funded by state allocations or by private endowments and alumni contributions, are particularly large at elite colleges and universities. For example, Winston and Yen report that the 10% of public schools that offer the most generous subsidies actually support 94.5% of the total cost of producing their students' education; the 10% most generous private institutions subsidize 75.3% of their students' education. How much do students know about these subsidies, and how does information and thought about them affect judgments of fairness?

We explored these questions with students at an elite private liberal arts college in the northeast, at an elite private university in the southeast, and at flagship state universities in the same states as the two private schools. We first asked students to indicate how fair or reasonable they rated their schools' total student charges. They were also asked to estimate how much their schools spent for the total undergraduate experience of each student, considering all costs, including instruction, room and board, financial aid, athletics, health services, and the portion of services such as the library and computer center, buildings and grounds, and administration that supports instruction. Next, subjects were told the actual amount spent and the percentage of their educations that were subsidized by state funding or private endowments or gifts. The stated subsidy amounts were conservative estimates based on operating budgets and annual capital spending figures. In all cases they exceeded total student charges by an average of nearly 100%. Finally subjects were asked to rate the fairness of the charges again. In addition, students at the private schools were asked the same questions about the public school in the same state and vice-versa.

The results for all four groups of subjects were remarkably consistent. First, students generally rated their own school's charges as more "reasonable" than "unreasonable." Second, for the most part students underestimated the degree of subsidy, especially, at the private schools. While students at the private liberal arts college in the northeast understood that there was a subsidy, they underestimated its magnitude. Students at the other three schools thought that the private school they judged charged about $10,000 more than it spent per student, and thus was making a large profit on each one. Students did estimate that there was a degree of subsidy at the public schools, but in some cases they underestimated its size by as much as $12,000. Our major finding, however, was that when students were told about the degree of subsidy, which were actually somewhat higher in percent terms at the public schools, they rated the private school's charges as considerably more reasonable, while they did not change their judgment about the reasonableness of the public schools. In fact, the students at the two northeastern schools ended up rating those two schools, the public and the private, as being equally reasonable in their charges. All four groups of students ended up thinking that both schools' prices were more reasonable than unreasonable. Similar findings were obtained from a group of public school teachers in the northeast who were asked the same questions about the two northeastern schools.

Taken together, these findings suggest that students and school teachers have different conceptions of the finances of public versus private institutions of higher education. They are aware that state universities subsidize their students' educations. They understand that providing a publicly supported education is, in some measure, their institutions' role in society. Thus they do not judge their prices differently when they learn the amount of the subsidy, even if they underestimate it by a large amount. On the other hand, many people have a different view of private colleges and universities, including the students who attend them. They seem to believe that like other private enterprises, these schools make a profit. Such students think that these schools take in more per student than they spend. When students learn about these substantial subsidies, they judge the schools' prices as more reasonable. Clearly there is a story to tell that many private colleges and universities are not getting across.

WHERE STUDENTS THINK THE MONEY GOES

It is unsettling that so many subjects begin with such little information about college financing. When students indicate that a private college spends much less per student than it charges, do they really think that the school is making a profit on each student, and saving the money, or using it for noneducational purposes? Obviously if students think that schools take in more from students than they spend on each student, they have little idea of the way the economics of higher education works. But it might help us get a clearer idea of what thoughts people do have by asking them specifically what they think happens to the money that the schools take in from each student, if that amount exceeds what they believe it spends on them. We studied this question with students at a New England private liberal arts college and a New England state university. Subjects were asked to estimate how much both their own school and the other school charged each student, and how much they thought each school spent per student to provide the total undergraduate experience. If they thought the amount spent was more than the charges, they were asked where the extra funding came from. If they thought the amount spent was less than the charges, they were asked where the unspent money collected from each student went. What was it used for?

Forty-five percent of the subjects at the private college believed that the college charged more than it spent, and 81% of the subjects at the public university felt the same about their school. Interestingly, this group of public university students was much less aware of the state subsidy than the students in our earlier studies, but we really do not know why. There are quite likely year-to-year variations in the kind of information students receive about the finances of their institutions. In any case, many students believed that their schools charged them more than it spent on them. Where did they think the extra money went? Among private school students, the most noted uses for the excess funds were building and grounds maintenance, new construction, faculty salaries and "overpaid executives," financial aid, recruiting and advertising, emergencies, and helping the local community. These responses indicate that subjects are thinking about the costs of producing the undergraduate experience in a limited way. They realize that more money is actually spent than what they report goes toward producing the undergraduate experience. They simply think of some of these expenditures and costs as not related to their experience. However, not all the subjects who report that they believe they pay a higher price than the actual cost simply think that additional funds are being spent elsewhere. Twenty-five percent of them believe that more money is being taken in than is being spent in total, and that the unspent funds are saved and invested, to add to the endowment. That is, significant numbers of private college students believe that the college builds its endowment by overcharging students, rather than using the endowment to subsidize their experience.

At the public university, students who think they are charged more than is spent on their experience typically mention athletics as the place where extra funds are diverted. They also mention in significant numbers administration, salaries, new programs, and campus beautification. Many of these students are quite bitter and sarcastic in their discussion of college finances. Like the majority of the private college students, they do not think that the university actually spends less per student than it charges. Rather, they believe that the funds are directed toward areas that have little to do with the total undergraduate educational experience.

JUDGING WHAT'S REASONABLE VS. WHAT'S TOO MUCH

In view of many students' limited understanding of the way college education is funded, we decided to try to get a clearer idea of their basis for assessing student charges. We asked them to judge the amount they were being charged along the dimension of "fair and reasonable" or "too much." In general, their responses were a bit closer to "too much" than to "fair and reasonable," but individual responses varied considerably. We also asked them to list the factors they considered in deciding how reasonable those charges were. At the private school, the most frequently mentioned considerations were family income, what other schools charged, the quality of their current experience, both curricular and extracurricular, and their future earning potential. Students felt that charges were too high in relation to family income, but not in relation to the quality of their experience, the cost of other schools, and the very high potential for future earnings that would come with their degree. Students rarely mentioned the rate of increase in the price for college in relation to other prices. In fact, some reported that college prices should be judged as a unique kind of expense. Most students felt that charges were completely fair in relation to these considerations, and they had no problem with them. Some felt frustrated by the high price, but still felt it was fair. A smaller portion were very angry and frustrated by the price, and felt it was too high.

At the public university, students judged reasonableness in terms of family income and the quality of their educational experience. Since they felt their families, most of them described as middle class, were hard-pressed to pay tuition bills, and since they were somewhat less than completely satisfied with their educational experience, their feelings about the justifiability of the high price were more skeptical and negative. Also, they were much less likely to think in terms of future earning potential. Finally, they mentioned frequently that their university's charges were much higher than those of other state universities around the country.

Considering both groups of students, it seems that ability to pay, the quality of experience, what other similar schools are charging, and—for the private school subjects—future earning potential are the key considerations. With these factors in mind, most students feel that while the price may be too high, it is worth paying. That is, they seem to feel that the price is both fair and reasonable on the one hand and too much on the other. How they balance those two perceptions determines their overall feeling about the fairness of the charges they are asked to pay, and ultimately, it seems, their overall evaluation of the institution that asks them to pay those charges.

WOULD STUDENTS BE WILLING TO PAY LESS AND GET LESS?

Our results show that students clearly think about the reasonableness of what they pay in terms of what they get. But that is not the only consideration. Even if they feel that they get a great deal, and what they get is fairly priced, if they also feel that they or their families simply cannot afford their education, then they believe that the price is too much. Do these findings mean that students would feel better about the price if it were lower, but they correspondingly got less for it? Perhaps they feel that their colleges are charging for—and delivering—a Cadillac quality education, but that they would prefer to pay for, and get, a Buick or even a Chevrolet level education. We thought it was worth asking them.

Our first study to explore this question asked subjects to rate the reasonableness of the price of their college before and after they received subsidy information. We also asked them after their initial reasonableness rating to indicate what they thought student charges at their school should be. We then asked them to consider the consequences of either increasing the charges and adding faculty and other services, or decreasing the charges and making cuts. Specifically, based on work done by a "priorities and resources" committee on one of the campuses, subjects were told that a student-faculty-administration committee had considered the consequences of raising or lowering student charges by $1,000 at the private university or by $300 at the public university. We explained that if support from the school were not changed, then the school's budget would be augmented or cut by 2% and that there would be corresponding additions or subtractions to faculty staffing levels, financial aid, support in the center for computing, the library and audiovisual services, and maintenance funds.

The subjects considered first the adds and then the cuts, or vice-versa, and indicated how willing they were to increase the price in exchange for the increase in services, or decrease the price in exchange for cuts in services. Then subjects were asked again to rate the reasonableness of the student charges and to indicate a second time what they thought the price for a year in college should be The subjects were quite disinclined to cut tuition if doing so would mean a loss of faculty, financial aid, computer support, etc. Interestingly, they were significantly more willing to increase the price if doing so meant adding faculty and services. That is, they indicated a moderate willingness to increase the price and add, but a distinct unwillingness to lower the price and cut. It seems clear that while students think that the price they are being charged is somewhere between "fair and reasonable" and "too much," they express great reluctance to set a lower price if they get less for it.

Of considerable interest was the students' answer to the final question about what students believe their schools should be charging. Recall that this question had been asked at the beginning of the survey as well, just after students first rated the reasonableness of the school's price. Students at the public school raised their recommended price at the end of the survey from about $7,300 to $9,700, just a few hundred less than the actual price of $10,000. Similarly, students at the private college raised their recommended price from $21,900 to $25,000. They were still not recommending the actual price of about $28,000, but they were much closer to it.

The increases in recommended price are intriguing. They come on the heels of both learning about the school's subsidy and considering their willingness to accept cuts for a reduction in tuition and additions with an increase in tuition. Which of these exercises leads people to raise their suggested price? Is it learning about the subsidy, or is it considering possible adds and cuts? Is it possible that both affect perceptions separately, or is the combination important? A further study was undertaken to answer this question.

INFORMATION ABOUT SUBSIDIES, ADDS, AND CUTS: THE IMPACT ON RECOMMENDED PRICES

The next studies of perceived reasonableness and recommended prices were also conducted at a private college and a state university, but in a different manner than those just described. The previous studies were conducted in laboratories where all the information was provided orally, sometimes with supporting overheads. Subjects wrote all the information they were given orally on answer sheets. This procedure maximized the extent to which subjects paid attention to the information we provided and the questions we asked about that information. The studies took 15 to 20 minutes each. The present research was conducted in student dormitories or during classes. Students were asked if they would take five minutes to complete a survey. It should be noted that since students were simply reading and answering a survey, there was some risk that the whole procedure would have less impact and capture less of their limited attentional resources. Still, it seemed worthwhile to find out if this potentially less involving approach would still generate enough reflection to affect student judgments.

There were two versions of the survey. The subsidy version first asked subjects to rate the reasonableness of the 1997-98 sticker price for their school, $29,350 for the private college or $10,000 for the state university. Then subjects were asked to report what their school should be charging and to estimate the amount spent per student for the total undergraduate educational experience. Then, after the actual cost information was given, they were asked to again rate the reasonableness of the actual charges and to recommend the amount that should be charged. The add/cut version of the survey explained to subjects the adds or cuts in faculty and services that would accompany a $300 or $1,000 increase or decrease in tuition (for the public or private school, respectively), assuming no change in college support. It also asked subjects for their rating of the reasonableness of the sticker price and their suggested charges figure both before and after they considered their willingness to make adds and cuts in exchange for increases and decreases in tuition.

At both schools, subsidy subjects increased their reasonableness rating in ways that were similar to past studies. Even though they participated in a procedure which commanded less of their attention, they still rated the total charges figure as significantly more fair and reasonable after learning the extent of college support for their undergraduate experience. Also, at the private college, students raised their recommended price from $24,900 to $26,400, an increase of about $1,500. At the state university, students raised their recommended price more than $900, from about $8,400 to $9,300.

The add/cut subjects, who considered possible adds and cuts and the corresponding $1,000 or $300 increase or decrease in charges, increased their reasonableness rating of the total charges figure to very much the degree as the subsidy version subjects. These students also raised their recommended price. At the private college there was an impressive increase of $2,500, from $24,600 to $27,100. At the state university, the increase was $450, from $7,800 to $8,250. In short, the exercise of asking private college students to consider the consequences of raising or lowering tuition without changing college support for the budget has an effect by itself very much like the effect of asking them to judge student charges in light of subsidy information.

THINKING ABOUT THE ECONOMICS OF HIGHER EDUCATION AND JUDGING STUDENT CHARGES

Taken together, the results of these studies suggest that while students react to the price of college with some degree of ambivalence and tend to see it as slightly too high, at least two procedures that make them think a little more seriously about college finances change their perceptions, several thousand dollars worth. One important implication is that students know very little about the economics of higher education. Most of them think that schools charge more than they spend on the undergraduate experience. A sizeable proportion think that schools make money from student charges that they use for investment, the construction of new buildings, or support for the community. Because students' opinions about the reasonableness of charges, or the ideal tuition, are based on such misinformation, it turns out that they are highly unstable and quite variable. One consequence of this instability is that anything that causes subjects to think about the realities of college finances can lead them to make more considered judgments about what charges are appropriate, and perhaps make them realize that they go to school in a complex environment that deserves more careful thought than heated emotion. In our research, we find that thinking about either the degree of college subsidy or the budgetary and programmatic consequences of raising or lowering tuition makes students recommend a higher sticker price. Our studies have identified one other particularly interesting indication of the extent to which student judgments about the reasonableness of charges can be affected by just a little bit of consideration of college finances. In two of our studies, after we asked subjects to estimate the amount that the institution spent to produce their experience, we asked them to indicate how reasonable they would rate the price charged if their cost estimate were correct. That is, they were asked to rerate the price after thinking about and estimating cost but before learning what the real cost was. At the private college, subjects judged the charges as significantly more fair and reasonable after simply estimating costs. This was more true for students who estimated that the college spent more than it charged than for students who thought it charged more than it spent, but it was true to some degree for both groups. Thus merely reflecting on the fact that schools have costs can increase reasonableness ratings.

One obvious but notable aspect of all the findings discussed here is that all of the procedures we use to ask students to think about college finances lead them in the same direction: to judge student charges as more reasonable. Perhaps there are other thoughts that could lead them in the other direction: to rate charges as less fair and reasonable. Students are certainly capable of becoming more outraged than they are now. But it may be that a range of things that they learn about the realities of the economics of higher education will lead them to judge student charges as more fair and reasonable. Further research awaits this issue.

REFERENCES

Jacoby, J. (1997). Money-making U. *The Boston Globe.* Appearing in *The Berkshire Eagle,* February 7, 1997, p. A9.

Morganthau, T., & Nayyar, S. (1996, April 29). Those scary college costs. *Newsweek,* 127 (18), 52-56.

Winston, G. C., & Yen, I. C. (1995). *Costs, subsidies, and aid in U.S. higher education.* Williamstown, MA: Williams Project on the Economics of Higher Education, Discussion Paper No. 32.

ACKNOWLEDGMENTS

Funding for this paper was provided by the Andrew Mellon Foundation through the Williams Project on the Economics of Higher Education. We thank Ethan Lewis and Lindsay Tucker for their help in conducting the research herein reported, and Gordon Winston for his overall guidance and support.

3

Opportunity and Responsibility: The Market For Selective Private Higher Education

James S. Roberts

Public debate remains intense about the value and affordability of higher education, particularly selective private education for undergraduates. Deep applicant pools and relatively high public confidence are coupled with frequently voiced concerns about affordability and accountability for the way we do our work as educators, scholars, and administrators. The discussion that follows draws upon a variety of recent studies to provide a perspective that is both market-oriented and sensitive to the distinctiveness of our particular business, higher education. While market perspectives and "knowing the business" inevitably go hand-in-hand in the for-profit commercial world, the same association in the nonprofit context may appear more novel. Nevertheless, Duke University, like all leading institutions of private higher education, operates in a very demanding and distinctive market context.

The premise of this discussion is that keeping the structure and dynamics of this market constantly in view is essential to our ability to sustain our leadership mission in higher education as we make strategic decisions about investment in quality programs and the prices students pay to participate in them. These decisions must also be framed, however, in light of commitments to accessibility and forms of accountability different from those found in commercial firms. These commitments are equally important to our mission.

The General Argument: The Market We're In

There is a real market for higher education in the United States, a market that offers educational opportunities to meet almost every taste, talent, and pocketbook. There are 2,215 four-year institutions of higher education in the United States, almost three-quarters of them private. About 5.7 million full-time undergraduates attend these institutions. In contrast to the educational systems in many other major industrial societies, which are dominated by national systems of public universities, America's mix of public and private institutions reflects its history of federalism and the broad scope afforded to religious denominations and other voluntary associations in shaping American society. The result is a market of national, regional, and local institutions of immense variety encompassing research universities and liberal arts colleges, public and private, large and small, rural and urban, denominational and independent. Given this diversity, any discussion of selective private higher education must begin with a clear understanding of its distinctive role in the broader market for higher education. Gordon Winston and colleagues in the Williams Project on the Economics of Higher Education, an interdisciplinary collaboration supported by the Andrew W. Mellon Foundation, have provided the conceptual framework for this kind of market analysis. Selective private higher education is the high cost/high value segment of American higher education.

Very few students in American higher education pay the full cost of the education they receive.[1] This is not because some students receive financial aid and some students don't, but because of substantial institutional subsidies available equally to all students, regardless of the price they pay. Institutional subsidies derive from state appropriations and, to a lesser degree, charitable gifts in the case of public institutions and from historically accumulated endowments and substantial philanthropy in the case of private institutions. In both cases, students enjoy the use of extensive facilities and academic resources like libraries and museums not fully financed out of current revenue. These institutional subsidies are much more significant economically than the subsidies distributed to specific individuals in the form of financial aid.

Total subsidy resources and total income from students determine the total amount invested in education; i.e., expenditure per student or the cost of education. For a given level of institutional subsidy, colleges and universities can choose either to keep prices low, in which case total investment in education approximates the level of institutional subsidy, or to charge significant sums, in which case the total investment in educational quality can substantially exceed the income available from either institutional subsidies or students alone. Most state institutions hew to the former strategy, while most private institutions follow the latter.

The different mixes between institutional subsidy and price to the student create a hierarchy of value in American higher education. Using aggregate institutional data available through the National Center for Educational Statistics of the US Department of Education, Winston and Yen have analyzed this hierarchy of value by comparing the prices students pay, both before and after financial aid, to the cost of the education they receive; i.e., to educational expenditures per student. All students receive an institutional subsidy if the cost per student exceeds the price per student. Winston and Yen calculated the institutional subsidy per student for all US institutions, then organized the data in order from the highest 10% to the lowest 10% in terms of institutional subsidy per student. While students in all groups receive subsidies to some degree, the institutional subsidies per student are greatest in those institutions that also charge the highest prices to students. In fact, students in the highest price group actually pay a lower percentage of the cost of their education than do students in lower price ranges. The value of what they receive in comparison to the price they pay is correspondingly the highest. According to Winston and Yen's calculations based on 1991 national data, the average educational expenditure per student in the top 10% of private institutions was $28,061, while the average tuition charge was $10,448. On average, therefore, students in this group received an institutional subsidy of $17,613 before any consideration of financial aid.[2] In the bottom 10%, students literally got what they paid for, and tuition charges and expenditures per student were virtually equal. Between the bottom and top, a market hierarchy is clearly evident in the relationship between the prices students pay and the economic value of the education they receive.

The best students attend the high price/high value institutions. Indeed, there is considerable excess demand to be admitted to these institutions. Institutions do not respond like rational business firms by expanding supply but by exercising a distinctive ability to choose their customers, based in part on the value they will add back to the educational enterprise. Thus there is an important feedback loop in the upper echelon of American private higher education. On the one hand, top tier institutions attract the best students because of the ability to invest in and provide an educational environment (residential facilities, small classes, etc.) that takes maximum advantage of student quality as an input in the educational process. On the other hand, the best students want to study with the best of their peers and with the best faculty. The dynamics of what economists Robert Frank and Philip Cook have called a "winner take all" market are in place, and indeed, the proportion of the very best students studying at the best institutions has increased over time (Frank & Cook, 1995).

The ability to attract the very best students at the most selective colleges and universities is thus associated with a combination of large institutional subsidies and high prices. This is a high value market segment, however, both because the subsidy/price ratio is high and because of the desirability of studying with the best students and the best faculty. On a national scale, the market is very small. Only about 25% of America's 18 to 24 year olds attend four-year colleges, and less than 1% of these students are enrolled in institutions charging tuition of $20,000 or more per year.[3] The highly selective colleges and universities that comprise the Consortium on Financing Higher Education (COFHE) enroll just 125,000 of the 5.7 million full-time undergraduates in the United States.[4]

ACCESS AND AFFORDABILITY:
ABILITY TO PAY AND THE ROLE OF FINANCIAL AID

Despite the high economic value associated with the high prices typical of selective private higher education—and the long queues of students seeking admission—there is substantial concern about the affordability and accessibility of elite private higher education. (This concern is sometimes conflated with concerns about the fundamental value and management effectiveness of higher education, which I will discuss later.) The concern about affordability is rooted largely in widely publicized analyses of the rate of growth of tuition charges in relationship to changes in national benchmarks such as the consumer price index and median family income. The fact that the cost of attending private institutions has grown at about twice the rate of inflation since the early 1980s, while median family income has been stagnant, gives rise to legitimate questions about the affordability of higher education particularly in the private sector (Clotfelter, 1996). These trends are the source of deep frustration and anxiety for many parents because they understand that access to the best colleges and universities pays greater rewards than ever before. From the point of view of private colleges and universities, with necessarily longer institutional memories, the tuition increases of the 1980s generated resources for new investments in educational quality following a decade during which tuition increases barely kept pace with inflation.[5] While eagerly seizing the opportunity to make these investments, leaders of selective institutions have never lost sight of the issue of affordability and access. A market perspective on the demand for selective private higher education can shed useful light on these issues.

Although median family income has been essentially stagnant over the last two decades, we have just been through a period (and may still be in a period) of major shifts in the distribution of income in the United States. As Frank and Cook note, for example, "the incomes of the top 1% [of US wage earners] more than doubled in real terms between 1979 and 1989, a period during which median income was roughly stable and in which the bottom 20% of earners saw their incomes actually fall by 10%" (Frank & Cook, 1995). Recent Census Bureau studies indicate that the share of national income available to the top 20% of families increased from 41.1% in 1974 to 43.5% in 1984 and to 46.9% in 1994. The share of income available to all other quintile groups declined. The top 5% commanded 15.5% of the income in 1974, 16% in 1984, and 20.1% in 1994 (Weinberg, 1996).

This shift in income distribution is highly correlated with educational attainment. According to data published in *Postsecondary Education OPPORTUNITY,* for example, "between 1978 and 1995 real median family income for families headed by individuals with one to three years of high school decreased by nearly 30%. During this same period real median incomes of families headed by persons with five or more years of college increased by nearly 25%" (1996, October).

There are several implications of this data for the market for selective private higher education:

- For a substantial portion of families most likely to send their children to highly selective private institutions, growth in income (and net assets) has probably kept pace with the growth in tuition charges.[6]

- Returns to investments in higher education have never been higher. Median family income across the entire US population is $36,751 for high school graduates, $61,780 for college graduates, $90,463 for individuals with PhDs, and $96,935 for individuals with professional degrees *(Postsecondary Education OPPORTUNITY,* 1996).[7] Expected lifetime earnings are correspondingly differentiated. These figures do not distinguish by type of educational experience, but there is reason to believe that these results would be further differentiated by the nature and selectivity of the institutions attended.[8] As a recent Moody's market assessment notes, "the perception of value returned from an investment in higher education is ultimately the most significant market factor. ... Indeed, the response of customers ... to higher education pricing demonstrates characteristics of demand for investment goods—the higher the price, the more the expectation of return and the greater the demand."[9]

- Universities themselves are dependent on the labor markets that are creating these differential rewards for highly trained specialists. Because we are so labor intensive in teaching, research, and many support functions, the costs of continuing to produce the same level of educational quality cannot easily be held to CPI, the measure most in the minds of the popular writers on higher education and the general public. In particular, the market for the most talented faculty is highly competitive. After declining in real terms during the 1970s, faculty salaries rose significantly faster than CPI in the 1980s (Clotfelter, 1996). By the early 1990s, inflation-adjusted salaries had begun to surpass the level of the early 1970s. The rate of increase has since slowed, but we can expect that compensation increases will continue to exceed CPI at the most selective institutions as they seek to attract and retain the most talented faculty members in a nationally and internationally competitive market.

■ Need-based financial aid programs are especially critical in selective private higher education. As Duke President Nannerl O. Keohane remarked in her most recent annual address to the faculty, this is a matter simultaneously of principle and prudential self-regard. Despite (or perhaps better, because of) the obvious reality that the most distinguished private universities are in the business of preparing leaders for the most significant arenas of public life, universities must be champions of the principle of "the career open to talent."

■ Need-based financial aid is an essential component of this principle because it allows highly selective institutions to choose a student body of quality and breadth of background without regard to individual financial circumstances. As already discussed, this freedom to select the best students is a key ingredient in the set of dynamics that enhances educational quality and sustains the market position of the best institutions. Prudentially, a genuine commitment to need-blind admissions and meeting full need may be the best answer to those who worry about the "sticker shock" of today's college costs.

■ While outwardly indistinguishable, the financial aid commitments of top tier institutions have little in common with the "tuition discounting" that weaker institutions are forced to practice to fill otherwise empty seats. For the most selective institutions, with their long waiting lists, a need-based financial aid policy is instead a corollary of the ability to choose their "customers" in the interests of maximizing the effectiveness of the educational process for the benefit of all students.

■ The question of affordability for "middle income" families is a particular concern, especially for families who receive little financial aid under current formulas and who cannot easily tap current income or accumulated assets to fund the costs of an expensive private higher education. The term "middle income melt" gained currency in the 1980s, reflecting the fear that expensive private institutions would lose increasing numbers of the best students to public institutions. This does not appear to have been the case, in part because public institutions, governed ultimately by the decisions of state legislatures, have been simultaneously decreasing their expenditures and increasing their tuition charges, eroding the price/value relationship at many institutions. The most recent national examination of this issue by Michael McPherson and Morton Schapiro (both affiliated with the Williams Project) actually found a slight increase in the probability that middle income families would enroll their children in private institutions over the last 15 years.[10]

In summary, a market perspective on the economics of higher education suggests the following: The most selective private institutions constitute a market segment in the world of higher education in which demand far exceeds supply (witness selectivity indicators), supply is relatively fixed (institutions do not want to become less selective and there are high barriers to entry in the form of substantial endowments and investments in physical plant), and a substantial proportion of the clientele whom we admit are from families willing and able to pay the prices we charge, which can be justified both in terms of the high value students receive for their tuition payments (institutional subsidies that represent the difference between cost per student and price per student) and the differential earnings they will experience having attended a top tier private institution. However, since, as Winston observes, we are peculiar in that we obtain one of our key inputs from our customers—namely student quality—we do not admit more and more students, which would dilute quality and our investment per student. Instead, we provide substantial financial aid to reinforce our ability to select the best qualified students. This commitment not only reinforces quality, a key factor in the economic model previously discussed, it also satisfies nonbusiness commitments to principles such as access and social diversity.

NOBODY'S BUSINESS:
MANAGEMENT AND ACCOUNTABILITY

Nobody owns a university. Gordon Winston, whose insights have informed this discussion, has noted that one of the principal factors distinguishing nonprofits from conventional businesses is the fact that they do not have owners. Because they do not have owners, nonprofits do not distribute the financial fruits of their labors; all resources are either consumed or reinvested for future use. And also because they do not have owners, nonprofits do not have the same clarity of accountability as business firms. Nonprofits, in the current jargon, have stakeholders rather than owners, a significant set of reasonably well-defined constituencies each of which has a legitimate but partial interest in the activities of the organization. University stakeholders include students, faculty, employees, alumni, prospective students, donors, employers, accrediting agencies, government and community leaders, sports fans, and the many potential beneficiaries of faculty research. The interests of these constituencies are not always fully congruent; balancing their interests under a long-term strategic vision is a major challenge for university administrators and trustees.

The fact that universities are "nobody's business" in the most literal sense (no one owns them) has allowed them historically to behave as though what they do is "nobody's business" in the figurative sense, that they are above conventional forms of accountability. Responding to public anxiety, much of it from the middle class, about access to the best institutions, journalists and trustees are demanding greater accountability. Regional accrediting bodies and higher education associations have taken up the theme with gusto.[11]

The intersection of public concerns about escalating prices for college attendance and the related demands for greater accountability have thrown a particularly glaring light on the nation's most expensive, elite institutions. In the most cynical *ProfScam* view, professors are being paid more to do less as administrators create bloated bureaucracies and eschew all responsibility for guiding educational outcomes toward socially constructive objectives.[12] In this view, the fact that we start with the best students and end with the best students is largely unrelated to the work done at these leading institutions. While clearly exaggerated, this caricature has seized part of the public imagination—more, thankfully, in the rhetoric of journalists and politicians than in the minds of those actually making decisions about their own and their children's education.[13]

What must be done to address the legitimate core of these concerns in a business-like way? There are four principal areas in which universities are adapting tools and concepts from business in order to improve their effectiveness and demonstrate their accountability within the contexts of their own distinctive missions and organizational cultures:

Increasing administrative efficiency. Virtually all universities are now engaged in major efforts to reduce their administrative costs, through a combination of process "reengineering" and investments in new information technology. The internal culture of centralized control, with "checkers checking checkers" is giving way to an organizational culture of more decentralized responsibility and independence, with more after-the-fact monitoring to ensure compliance with institutional policies and the numerous regulatory requirements under which institutions of higher education labor.

Concentrating resources in areas of greatest comparative advantage. In a period of shrinking resources, virtually every institution is focusing its management attention on the question "what can we do uniquely well?" in serving individual students, generating productive research and scholarship, and—more broadly—in differentiating itself in the competition for key ingredients of excellence in higher education: the best faculty and students and access to external resources.

Strengthening "customer focus." Concerns about cost and accountability have created a renewed emphasis on the fundamental importance of providing an education of outstanding quality, particularly to undergraduates. While some members of the academic community object to the term "customer," its emergence in the vocabulary of higher education is an important indication of a growing sophistication and assertiveness on the part of parents and students in demanding both educational quality and responsive administrators at all levels. Institutions are responding in ways ranging from reexamining the undergraduate curriculum and faculty teaching commitments to improving registration systems and student billing.

Focus on "value added" activities. Institutions are examining their curricula and their resource deployment to direct resources to "value adding" activities. Since the "value" in an educational institution is not reducible to market share, net income, or stock values, the issues involved are inherently complex. But the question of what adds value is being asked, and efforts to define objectives more clearly and find appropriate ways to monitor and measure outcomes inevitably follow.

A MONSTER UNDER THE BED?
NEW FORMS OF COMPETITION

In the earlier discussion about the distinctive characteristics of the market for selective private higher education, the observation was made that demand has continued to outstrip supply despite the rapid increase in college costs. On the demand side, this phenomenon is bolstered by trends in the nation's distribution of wealth, which rewards the skills and credentials higher education confers to an extent unprecedented in the nation's history. The "winner take all" phenomenon, reinforced by the recent prominence of national ranking schemes, makes the very best institutions all the more popular. The combination of rising real incomes for those segments of the population most likely to send their children to selective private institutions and substantially increased investments in financial aid have supported this demand despite rising costs. On the supply side, selective institutions do not expand to meet demand in order to continue to control student quality. At the same time, substantial barriers to entry, particularly in the accumulation of endowment and physical plant, prevent newcomers from encroaching on the market for top students.

Is this favorable demand relationship, which apparently favors a small number of well-established, high-quality, high-cost institutions, likely to last? Several factors are worth considering.

On many fronts, the top tier private institutions have the capability to adapt and evolve in response to changing public needs that could affect their market position. For example, institutions are responding to public concerns about academic accountability, reexamining the balance between teaching and research and between undergraduate and graduate education. This reexamination is unlikely to result in wholesale changes in private higher education, but rather to refine the balances and, perhaps more importantly, allow us to think creatively about how to take best advantage of the many potential synergies among these major dimensions of institutional life.

Aggregate demand for American private higher education will remain strong. The economic and social forces that have created increasing demands for well-educated "knowledge workers" over the last two decades show no sign of abating. The special challenges of providing public and private sector leadership in today's environment of global competition, rapid technological change, and enduring challenges to the principles of social justice will continue to require the breadth and depth of knowledge available in the great institutions of American higher education. In terms of sheer numbers, the Department of Education predicts that enrollments in private four-year colleges will increase at an average annual rate of about 1.7% per year over the next decade.[14]

Public institutions, which currently enroll about two-thirds of the nation's four-year college students, will continue to be the numerically predominant force in American higher education. State legislators understand the importance of higher education to the welfare of their citizens and the fortunes of their states, but competing demands for limited resources have reduced the rate of investment in higher education and have led to rates of tuition increase higher than in the private sector. Over the last 15 years, state investments in higher education per $1,000 of personal income have decreased nearly 30% (*Postsecondary Education OPPORTUNITY*, 1995). While we can all hope that the major flagship campuses of the historically great public university systems retain their strength, there seems to be no reason to expect that these institutions will sap the strength of the leading private institutions given reasonable cost constraint and continuing investments in quality, often through successful external fundraising.

New technologies are creating the possibility of new forms of education, the university without walls or Cyber U. Creating a virtual university is technically feasible, as has already been demonstrated by the emerging Western Governors' University. One can imagine such a university as the *ne plus ultra* of the "winner take all" principle in higher education. Cyber U could have *all* the best faculty and *all* the best students, all linked seamlessly in a highly efficient network. Perhaps a for-profit enterprise,[15] Cyber U might boast a student to faculty ratio of 1,000:1 or more. Many current teaching posts would be threatened. Is some more moderate version of this scenario a threat to selective private higher education? It seems unlikely. Certainly such enterprises, whether public or private, may come into being. It is also likely that new technologies will continue to make their way into the teaching repertoire of the faculty. Technology will also undoubtedly play an increasing role in post-graduate professional training for working adults. But education in the fullest sense is a function of sustained interactions of minds and personalities, of students with the faculty and their peers, and is thus intimately connected to place, scale, and tradition.[16] American higher education offers great variety in all these respects and many more: There is a true market in which students make real choices and match their talents, needs, and resources to the market. There is currently no reason to believe that those institutions which are most successful now will be fundamentally threatened by Cyber U as long as they are flexible and creative in adapting new technologies to their own needs and purposes.

The conclusion that the market for selective private higher education is unlikely to be successfully contested by currently unknown rivals placing big bets on Cyber U does not mean that there will not be significant changes within this market. Competition is intense within the high price/high value market segment for all factors of educational quality: resources, faculty, and students. Because of the different histories and access to donative capital, the playing field is far from level. The strongest may be getting relatively stronger, with a "winner take all" dynamic within the top echelon that is a grave threat to some weaker institutions trying desperately to reverse an expenditure per student/student quality dynamic that is unwinding. Indeed, it speaks volumes about the nature of this market that at least one well-known private university has set a strategic course out of its current financial woes by downsizing its undergraduate class, precisely to increase selectivity and student quality. Even among the more secure members of the high cost/high value market, technological change and globalization will stimulate innovations that present opportunities as well as challenges. In particular, it is likely that new forms of local, national, and global partnerships among institutions of higher education (and perhaps other kinds of institutions as well) will evolve in this environment, many of which will be aided by the new technologies. Partnerships will result both from the interest in all major institutions in internationalizing their programs and from the business logic of focusing locally on areas of comparative advantage. Institutions with strong "brand names" will be in an advantageous position to set the terms of these partnerships.

A major reconstruction of the transition from adolescence to adulthood in American society would be required to alter fundamentally the picture presented here. An earlier integration of young adults into the labor force, for example, with more education and training conducted on the job or with periods of work and periods of education alternating over several years could undermine the current pre-eminence of a sustained, four-year education in a residential setting with age peers of similar talents and ambitions. Such an alternative pattern might well exploit distance learning technologies in facilitating the integration of work and study. Examples of this approach to education already exist, of course, in the form of work/study co-op programs such as those found at Northeastern University and Drexel and in current opportunities for remote education at an individual student's own pace. Will either of these models become the new paradigm? Again, it seems unlikely, barring some major economic cataclysm, that the current pattern of primary focus on post-secondary education in the 18- to 24-year-old age span will change. An alternative paradigm would seem to depend either on vast improvements in our primary and secondary school systems or the willingness of American business to take on the functions of educating society. Since American business seems to want people capable of lifelong learning rather than individuals trained for the needs of the moment, the kind of liberal education offered at top tier private institutions seems unlikely to go out of style.

Affordability will remain a major issue of public policy and institutional focus. The rate of increase in college costs has now slowed to levels significantly below those of the late 1980s and early 1990s. At the federal level, support for the now familiar package of grant, loan, and work-study programs may be augmented or perhaps to some extent replaced by tax reforms like the educational IRA to promote college savings. At the institutional level, need-based aid will remain an important commitment among colleges and universities most committed to quality.

This section started with a question: Is the favorable demand relationship in the market for higher education, which apparently favors a small number of well-established, high-quality, high-cost institutions, likely to last? The answer developed here is, "yes, if": if we respond to legitimate concerns about academic accountability; if we incorporate new technologies and new markets; and if we continue to stress affordability in managing our costs, setting our price, and maintaining our financial aid commitments. This optimistic assessment is based on the conclusion that fundamental individual and social value is created when the best students and the best faculty are brought together with the right purposes and under the right conditions. The transformations that can take place are difficult to measure but nonetheless real. As Martin Trow has written:

> One of the major functions of higher education that evades all measurement is our ability to raise the horizons of our students, to encourage them to set their ambitions higher than if they had not come under our influence. Colleges and universities at their best teach students that they can actually have new ideas, ideas of their own rather than merely collections of

ideas produced by others. That is not a conception of self very often gained in secondary school, and yet it lies at the heart of most of what people who gain a post-secondary education achieve in their lives. No formal assessment measures this increased self-confidence and belief in one's capacity to think originally and effectively, yet can we doubt that it is one of the great goods that attaches to a university education?... More and more we see the importance of initiative, originality and the capacity to think in bold and fresh ways as a central element in success in the professions and in business enterprise.[17]

CONCLUSION: IMPLICATIONS FOR DUKE

The preceding discussion provides a general framework for thinking about the market for selective private higher education. By way of conclusion, it may be useful to locate a particular university—Duke University—more specifically in its market context.

■ Duke operates in the very small, high price/high value segment of the American higher education market.

■ An institution's success in this market segment depends on many factors. A threshold condition is the ability to invest substantially more in the education of each student than it charges in tuition, and a key measure of success is the ability to generate excess demand so that the institution can choose its customers based on quality. The longer an institution has been in a position to make such investments and select its students, the greater its reputational capital. Duke's ability to invest more in the education of each student than it charges in tuition is not as great as that of other top tier institutions, and its ability to attract the very best students remains less certain.

■ Marshaling resources to invest in academic programs that will attract and serve the best students depends on several factors. Controlling administrative costs, focusing resources based on comparative advantage, developing customer focus, and investing from a value-added framework are the *sine qua nons* of success in a world of increasingly constrained resources and increasing standards of accountability. Duke is addressing these issues through its academic and administrative planning, including the preparation of its reaccreditation self-study report on "Balancing the Roles of the Research University." On the revenue side, the key ingredients are tuition, endowment spending, and fundraising.

- Over the last decade, the leading private institutions made substantial new investments as tuition income grew much more rapidly than the CPI. Duke's investment in academic programs in arts and sciences and school of engineering grew at an average real rate of approximately 5.3% annually after providing for financial aid and academic and administrative support costs.[18] During that period, Duke increased the size and quality of its faculty in undergraduate programs; removed most first-year graduate students from independent instructional roles; created an all-freshman east campus; invested heavily in PC-based network computing; introduced automation into its libraries; improved facilities for instruction and research through new construction and a program of systematic classroom renovation; and increased the quality and diversity of the student body. The cumulative effect of these kinds of investments are recognized both in the quality and depth of our applicant pools and in the increased recognition we have received in National Research Council and *US News* rankings. These improvements were funded primarily by tuition, including two "two-tiered" step adjustments to provide revenue specifically to increase the size of the faculty, create funds for computing and facilities improvements, and provide funds for an effective program of financial aid. Duke deliberately reduced its endowment spending rate during this period to help ensure a firm foundation for the future.

- The rates of growth the most distinguished private institutions have enjoyed over the past decade are unlikely to be sustained in the years ahead. Nevertheless, investments in new programs and improved quality will continue. Such investments are both the means by which the most selective institutions distinguish themselves collectively from less prestigious institutions and the basis of competition with each other for the best faculty, students, and external funding opportunities. It is essential that Duke also be able to continue to make new investments in academic quality, and particularly in the quality of its undergraduate academic programs. Already we know that the average rate of tuition growth at private institutions has been reduced to about 5% for the last two years; and this national trend is also reflected among COFHE institutions, which include the nation's most selective private colleges and universities. As tuition differentiation among the leading institutions diminishes, the strength of endowment support for academic programs will make the critical difference. While we can be thankful that Duke has sufficient endowment power to allow us to operate in the premier market segment, our endowment per student is multiples smaller than that of a number of our most distinguished peers, all of whom are more or less constantly engaged in increasing their endowments even further.

■ Duke will probably never have the resources of some of those institutions, certainly not in our lifetimes. This does not mean we cannot be as good, but it does mean that we have to be more selective and more creative in managing our resources and our programs than better endowed institutions. To maintain our current position and pace of improvement will require a judicious combination of decisions regarding program investments, tuition levels, and endowment spending. Given current downward trends in tuition pricing, which are likely to be long-term, external fundraising and effective endowment management must be critical ingredients in our continuing success.

In summary, Duke University and a small number of other highly selective private institutions face a period of significant opportunity with a heightened sense of responsibility. Despite the harsh criticism and unflattering headlines of the last decade, student demand for selective private higher education has remained strong. Our graduates serve in key roles of public leadership and are rewarded as never before for their service to business enterprises and the professions. Gallup

Poll data indicate that public confidence in private higher education is high. Success in renewing and strengthening our leadership will require a shared commitment to responsibility and accountability in demonstrating effective management, preserving affordability and accessibility, and educating students effectively for lifelong learning, achievement, and service.

ENDNOTES

1) Much of what follows derives from: Winston, G. C., & Yen, I. C. (1995, July). *Costs, prices, and subsidies in U.S. higher education.* Williams Project on the Economics of Higher Education, Discussion Paper 32. Winston extends some of the insights from his work with Yen in another paper that explores the similarities and differences between for-profit and nonprofit business entities in "The Economic Structure of Higher Education: Subsidies, Customer-Inputs, and Hierarchy," a paper discussed at the October 1996 Stanford Forum on Higher Education Futures. I am grateful to Professor Winston for his willingness to continue an email dialogue with me about his work.

2) Winston & Yen, 1995, p. 27. The analysis is based on the Integrated Postsecondary Education Data System (IPEDS) maintained by the National Center for Education Statistics of the US Department of Education. Winston and Yen supplement the IPEDS data with their own analysis of capital costs, i.e., "'the rental rate' for the physical capital used in producing education at a given institution" (p. 9). Note that outlays for financial aid are not included in the pool of educational expenditures that constitute the institutional subsidy. According to this analysis, financial aid expenditures provided an additional, individual subsidy averaging $3,522 per student, decreasing the average net tuition charge to $6,926 and increasing the total average subsidy per student to $21,135.

3) Calculated from *The Chronicle of Higher Education Almanac.* (1996, September), 30.

4) Author's calculation. The COFHE membership includes Amherst College, Barnard College, Brown University, Bryn Mawr College, Carleton College, Columbia University, Cornell University, Dartmouth College, Duke University, Georgetown University, Harvard University, The Johns Hopkins

University, MIT, Mount Holyoke College, Northwestern University, Oberlin College, Pomona College, Princeton University, Rice University, Smith College, Stanford University, Swarthmore College, Trinity College, The University of Chicago, University of Pennsylvania, University of Rochester, Washington University, Wellesley College, Wesleyan University, Williams College, and Yale University.

5) See Clotfelter, p. 5 for an illuminating graph of the history of tuition charges at the University of Chicago and Duke University since 1890. The data is presented in constant 1991/92 dollars and indicates three periods of rapid real growth in tuition charges: the 1920s, the 1960s, and the 1980s.

6) Moody's Public Finance. (1995, January 13). Demographic outlook for higher education. *Perspective on Higher Education.* This market evaluation notes that "the ability of high-priced institutions to charge high tuition is probably better correlated with financial asset appreciation than with family income" (pp. 3-4) and demonstrates the strong correlation between the Dow Jones average and the rise of tuition in private institutions.

7) See also Clotfelter, p. 62.

8) See for example, Rumberger, R. W., & Thomas, S. L. (1993). The economic returns to college major, quality, and performance. *Economics of Education Review,* 12 (1) 1-19. See also Fox, M. (1993). Is it a good investment to attend an elite private college? *Economics of Higher Review,* 12 (3) 137-51.

9) Moody's Public Finance.

10) McPherson, M., & Schapiro, M. (1996, October). *Are we keeping college affordable?: The most recent data on student aid, access, and choice.* Paper presented at the Stanford Forum on Higher Education Futures, p. 7. McPherson is now president of Macalester College and Schapiro is Dean of Faculty at the University of Southern California.

11) For a thoughtful discussion of these issues, see Trow, M. (1996, March 21-23). *On the accountability of higher education in the United States.* Unpublished paper presented at the Princeton Conference on Higher Education, and later distributed to COFHE Assembly Representatives. Trow, who was coauthor of a recent study on accreditation sponsored by the Andrew W.

Mellon Foundation, is eloquent on the importance and forms of accountability—and the difficulty of measuring in any conventional sense the "outcomes" we hope for in the educational process at the university level. See also Graham, P. A., Lyman, R. W., & Trow, M. (1995, October). *Accountability of colleges and universities.* New York, NY: Columbia University.

12) Journalist Charles J. Sykes (1988) authored a widely cited book whose title epitomized the negative view of academic culture: *ProfScam: Professors and the demise of higher education.* Washington, DC: Regnery Gateway.

13) A recent Gallup Poll reported in the *Chronicle of Philanthropy* (1996, October 17) showed greater public confidence in "private colleges and universities" (p. 9) than in any other form of public organization. Fifty-seven percent of respondents indicated either "a great deal" or "quite a lot" of confidence in private educational institutions, and only 7.5% indicated "very little" confidence.

14) Calculated from *The Chronicle of Higher Education Almanac.* (1996, September), p. 18.

15) See for example Davis, S., & Botkin, J. (1994). *The monster under the bed: How business is mastering the opportunity of knowledge for profit.* New York, NY: Simon and Schuster.

16) At a recent conference I attended, the director of mathematics at IBM research labs was asked to what extent his firm relied on distance learning internally. His response highlighted this dichotomy. He said the Internet was used for "training" but not for "education," which takes place in face-to-face settings that promote personal interaction.

17) Trow, pp. 37-38.

18) Provost's office calculation of unrestricted "core expense" growth for compensation and operating expenses. The real growth rate was approximately 6.4% annually if sponsored research and restricted endowment income are included. See also Clotfelter's *Buying the Best* for discussions of expenditure growth at Chicago, Duke, Harvard, and Carleton.

REFERENCES

Clotfelter, C. T. (1996). *Buying the best: Cost escalation in elite higher education.* Princeton, NJ: Princeton University Press.

Frank, R. H., & Cook, P. J. (1995). *The winner take all society: Why the few at the top get so much more than the rest of us.* New York, NY: Penguin.

Postsecondary Education OPPORTUNITY. (1995, November).

Postsecondary Education OPPORTUNITY. (1996, October).

Sykes, Charles J. (1988). *ProfScam: Professors and the demise of higher education.* Washington, DC: Regnery Gateway.

Weinberg, D. H. (1996, June). A brief look at postwar US income inequality. *Current Population Reports.* US Census Bureau, with supporting table available via the World Wide Web.

Enabling Metaphors of Innovation and Change

Michael J. Kelly

The Stanford Higher Education Forum has had over the years one central theme: How do we go about changing our institutions? Through the courtesy of Bill Massy and Joel Meyerson we have been presented with analytical insight into the state of higher education as well as a wonderful array of metaphors of change: the downside of downsizing, the use of computer simulation games to understand interrelationships in higher education, tying evaluation of quality and distribution of resources in higher education in Great Britain, information technology as the stimulus for change and radical transformation of higher education, medical education as a model of what's coming for the rest of higher education, total quality management, etc. By metaphor I simply mean a framework for thinking about fundamental or key ideas that precipitate change, a way of thinking that captures the basic thrust and direction of our thinking and affects our practice and action. One of the metaphors that stands out most vividly in my mind from these sessions is Jim Duderstadt describing the college presidency as something not unlike the classic western gun fight: You strap on your guns and you go out and you do the job, knowing full well that one day you will meet up with a faster draw. Which all goes to show that metaphor and prophecy are closely connected. I'd like to pose an idea that is, I hope, at once friendly to and critical of the Massy-Meyerson collection of enabling metaphors, and at the same time constructive, something I trust you can put to use. How does one evaluate the saliency of different ideas as metaphors? That is an important question, if we view ourselves as agents of change. Change for what larger purpose? Change that transforms our institutions in precisely what ways? I propose to suggest a way of thinking about these questions that is both practical and directly connected to our particular situations. Let us begin with a thought experiment.

Think for a moment about the idea of writing biography. If I was to write your life story in, say, short story scale, it would be likely to have some basic data about when and where you were born and went to school, what your family is like, what your occupation is, maybe even such things as how much money you have made, where you have lived, when you retired, what positions or titles you held, and the like. But the basic point of a biography is to make some sense or coherence of it all. So a good story about you would probably include the values that motivated you and moved you through life, whether originating with your family or coming from the variety of crises you have had to face and overcome, your regrets, triumphs, problems you successfully solved or failed to solve, situations you did or did not resolve or extricate yourself from. The story makes sense of your life by making the biography telling; that is, it integrates many different facts and figures and motives and elements of character and action to try to capture fully and honestly the quality and essence of a lifetime.[1]

My first argument is that something similar—a kind of biography or story—can be written about an organization, amalgamating the facts and figures and the numbers of people involved, budgets, subunits, missions and goals, with elements of character—or institutional personality. It would cover the crises, challenges, way of treating its employees, and the people it serves. The story is analogous to a life story; that is, a good institutional biography would deal with what makes the organization tick, what motivates the people in the organization to stay together and work together (Selznick, 1957).

Writing a biography of the life of an institution or nonfictional story poses some interesting challenges. Where should one begin? Would an appropriate start, for example, be to sketch the main charactors, the real and the perceived leaders of the institution? Would they be senior faculty, selected administrators? The president? Certain key members of the board? Who are the other actors, the heroes, the villains, the forces that count, that contribute, get co-opted, or neutralized? If I am going to be writing a story of any interest or depth, wouldn't I want to write about significant crises or conflicts that the institution has experienced and dealt with either successfully or unsuccessfully? Surely the credibility of the narrative will be greatly strengthened by honesty—no need to indulge in brutal candor—about failures. I'd certainly have to talk about money and resources and the way they are allocated. I'd have to talk about constituencies or clients both within and outside of the institution and their perceptions of the place. And finally, I expect I would have to deal with the way the characters talk to each other, the style of communication within the institution. How formal is it, how informal? Are there conflicting patterns of communication? Do people feel in the loop or out of the loop? How big a rumor mill is the place? Is there a lot of unpleasantness or pleasantness in the style of discussion between deans and administrators, faculty and administration, students and staff? Is candor the rule of the day? Is it a passive-aggressive snakepit?

Now I want to take the thought experiment one step further: Thus far we've been thinking of writing history, thoughtful and rich description, a category of nonfiction. Now I want to extend it into the category of fiction, or perhaps more accurately, probable or conditional nonfiction. What if we were to extend the story line into the future, to try to connect the past, where we've come from, to our future projects? The advantage of thinking in terms of an institutional biography or story of the life of an institution projected into the future is that it imposes on you a certain discipline with a number of analytical advantages.

First, it requires you to think of a realistic vision of institutional growth and change that involves people and their places in the story, the complexities and character of the organization, the likelihood of conflict, and the central place of motivation, strategies, and counter-strategies for the story to move forward.

Second, because it is an open-ended description of the enterprise, it obviously has a wide range of possible beginnings, developments, and closings. It requires you to think about where the story is going, how to make it come to a coherent and satisfactory conclusion or end result, and whether the story is to end hopefully, or with, say, cynical resignation. The story can be rewritten as different events unfold. There obviously is no formula, no model, at least for a nonfiction story of this mixed fictional mode.

Third, if the story is not to be a dreadful James Michener production drowning in facts and figures and details, it forces you to integrate various elements of the narrative and point up important things and keeps you from focusing on trivial and less important elements in the life of the institution. A biography that is largely a list of accomplishments, like some presidents' letters to alumni I've seen, is not only dull but unuseful because it does not address issues of significance and forces that generate or prevent change. Because the story is about the character and life of an institution, in all likelihood, it is going to focus on fundamental values or fundamental characteristics of the institution and how these are changed or transformed or enriched as the life of the institution unfolds. This focus on fundamentals is, I believe, an extremely important advantage of this kind of framework.

Fourth, a good biography puts the person or institution in context. Organizations and individuals are creatures of their times, just as professionals are deeply impacted by the character and projects of their clients. In our case, the larger worlds of higher education and American society are fundamental to understanding the challenges and responses of our institutions.

Fifth, thinking in terms of the story forces one to confront a very basic question, beyond that of who the major characters are, namely who is writing this story? How wide is the group of authors? Can a good story be written by a committee? Who is the lead author?

Sixth, one of the most important benefits of thinking in terms of an institutional biography is that a compelling story has to have some affect, some emotion, connected to human motivations and feelings that are part of the story. This is one of the most powerful points of a wonderful little book by the Yale sociologist, Burton Clark, called *The Distinctive College,* a study of Antioch, Reed, and Swarthmore. First published in 1970, Clark talks about the kind of story I'm proposing here in terms of what he calls the "organizational saga." To Clark, a saga is more than the historical story, it is "a collective understanding of a unique accomplishment" that presents not only "some rational explanation of how certain means led to certain ends," but also the emotion that "turns a formal place into a beloved institution, to which participants may be passionately devoted." As Clark puts it, "the genesis and persistence of loyalty is a key organizational and analytical problem." "The most important characteristic, and consequence of an organizational saga," Clark argues, "is the capturing of allegiances, the committing of staff to the institution. Emotion is invested to the point where many participants significantly define themselves by the central theme of the organization" (1970).[2]

Clark's elevation of the organizational biography to the level of saga suggests another advantage of thinking in terms of the story of an institution: It encourages a tendency toward ambition, or at least a sense of historic framework, where initiatives fit into a larger context. What, for example, is the relevance of cost cutting? Is it a short-term move to facilitate a long-term strategy? How does it relate to a more expansive concept of the institution's future and identity? What is the larger institutional relevance of the technique, or goal of the change under contemplation? How does it fit? Is it coherent with the institution's sense of direction as a whole?

The term "whole" identifies another critical dimension of this nonfictional, quasifictional exercise—the choice of the frame of the story. The decision to write a narrative about the whole institution is a demonstrably more challenging task than an account, projected into the future, of a subunit—the law school, school of education, division of facilities, or the office of student financial aid. Burton Clark, in an article (1971) following up *The Distinctive College,* suggests that perhaps the way a large university captures the sense of distinctiveness and accompanying loyalty and trust, a characteristic of the small colleges he studied, is to encourage these qualities in decentralized units. Clark's unrestrained optimism about the unreservedly benign nature of distinctive subunits might get a decidedly mixed reception by certain actors in central administration.[3]

Clark raises an important question: Can one, in fact, write the institutional biography of a large American university? Is it feasible? Or must one deconstruct the enterprise into a set of smaller scale stories? Will the collection of stories come to have any overall coherence? Can a story be made of the whole? Do vast clinical health care businesses competing day-to-day in a turbulent market and federally financed research enterprises share anything like the same set of goals and assumptions as the core liberal arts academic program? Herman Hesse, in *Steppenwolf*, a pathbreaking novel/meditation first published in 1927, argued passionately against the coherent self: The self is divided, indeed hopelessly fractured, into scores of selves, a cacophony of interests and impulses. Contrast that with an ancient view, Aristotle's concept of the human person, as described by Anthony Kronman, Dean of Yale Law School (1987):

> It is ... important to discover which way of life is most likely to preserve a relation of fellow feeling or friendship, as Aristotle calls it, among the different parts of one's own self, some of which must necessarily be subordinated for the sake of others. A person whose soul has, in Aristotle's phrase, "friendly feelings" towards itself, a person whose parts are not openly at war or engaged in subtler contests of repression and revenge, possesses a quality of wholeness that is best described by the simple term "integrity."

We all know our organizations' sense of wholeness is affected by tensions between the devotees of scholarship and teaching, between alumni versus faculty visions for the institution, between the business and managerial people and the freer spirits on the faculty who believe financial considerations are a sellout to the forces of evil. An institutional biography must address, accommodate, or confront these tensions, including the question whether the assorted parts of the multiuniversity or university have a sufficient modicum of "friendly feelings" toward each other to qualify us to characterize our institutions as having "institutional integrity."

Is this idea of writing a story or narrative description or biography of your institution a practical idea, or a wholly theoretical exercise? Are there any examples? I don't have a precise model to offer you, in part because I think one of the advantages of this approach, unlike strategic planning, is that there are no formulas or models to follow in writing the kind of nonfiction and projected nonfiction that I have talked about. In all likelihood the work of Burton Clark is too ambitious in scope as an example to draw upon, although many of our institutions have some fine historical work that can be redacted and summarized and made intelligible as a basis for thinking about a projected future.

A number of law school and pre-law teachers use short story scale descriptions of law practices which lend themselves to a pedagogical approach of asking what is going to happen to this law practice in the future (Kelly, 1994). Stories don't require length to be effective. Indeed, there is a literature that I haven't yet addressed that underscores the enormous power of very short descriptive statements. I refer to Collins' and Porras' *Built to Last: Successful Habits of Visionary Companies* (1994) and their article (1996) in the *Harvard Business Review* that is something of a rewrite of a 1991 article in the *California Management Review*. They talk of the use of an exercise they call "vivid description" as a means of envisaging their future.

From their point of view, the classic vivid description is Henry Ford's:

I will build a motor car for the great multitude.... It will be so low in price that no man making a good salary will be unable to own one and enjoy with his family the blessings of hours of pleasure in God's great open spaces....When I'm through everybody will be able to afford one, and everyone will have one. The horse will have disappeared from our highways, the automobile will be taken for granted ... [and we will] give a large number of men employment at good wages.

Or Sony in 1950:

We will be the first Japanese company to go into the U.S. market and distribute directly...We will succeed with innovations that U.S. companies have failed at ... Fifty years from now, our brand name will be as well known as any in the world.... . 'Made in Japan' will mean something fine, not something shoddy.

Or a more current example from Jack Welch of General Electric:

> As we succeed in ridding our company of the tentacles of ritual and bureaucracy, we are now better able to attack the final and most difficult challenge of all. And that is the empowering of our...people, the releasing of their creativity and ambition, the direct coupling of their jobs with some positive effect on the quality of a product or service,...to see a connection between what he or she does all day and winning in the market place.... Small companies thrive and grow on that sense of contribution and reward. We want it as well, and everything we do to evolve our management system will be consistent with getting it (Collins & Porras, 1991).

I am calling for a more historically rooted description than Collins and Porras because I think it is far more suited to the kinds of institutions we represent, and far more effective as a device for clarifying our thinking and our goals. The organizational biography projected into the future is both a more organic and analytical exercise than Collins' and Porras' hyperventilating vivid descriptions or some of their other exercises like their highly charged Big Hairy Audacious Goals (BHAGs). But they are kissing cousins, or at least related to each other in the sense that concepts of change and strategies of implementation need to be related—if I can borrow a phrase from Charles Taylor (1991)—to a horizon of intelligibility or significance, some sense of what we want the institution to be, some visualization of our ideals. Thus, I think there is another distinct advantage to the institutional biography: It forces one to arrive at some sense of desired future for the institution against which to evaluate the metaphors of change being contemplated. This idea of writing the narrative of an institution into the future is, in important respects, a vision stimulating exercise.

Let me briefly comment on the distinction between the institutional biography and the standard modes of strategic planning that have been widely used and accepted in higher education. Tom Gilmore has, I think persuasively, argued that what he calls "loosely coupled systems" like universities and government agencies and other forms of nonprofit institutions are not really ideal subjects for strategic planning because the processes for change in higher education are not analogous to the corporate world. While strategic planning often has the value of informing a university community what the leadership endorses, it entirely ignores the subtleties of process and strategies of indirection and marginal opportunities to make a difference that an effective educational leader needs to exploit in order to make a difference in an institution.

A 20- to 30-page organizational biography thoughtfully describing an institution and the elements that are crucial to its character is an enormously ambitious undertaking. It is unlikely, because of the effort required to make it a finished product, to succeed as a practical method of helping us think clearly and cogently about effective and desirable strategies for change. But the concept can be useful if adapted as a thinking and planning exercise. Much of its value comes from framing or outlining what a good institutional biography should include. One could imagine a small group, each member of which is asked to outline the essential elements of the story of their institution up to the present. A group discussion of these various outlines could lead to a richer, more subtle and wide-ranging understanding of the institution than the work of a single "biographer." An even more stimulating dialogue and review of alternative strategies and visions for change would emerge from a second phase outline process extending the biography into the future.

It is not even clear to me that the institutional biography process needs to be a formal writing or written outline for discussion. Let me give you an example from my own institution in which nothing like writing or thinking about writing a story occurred, and yet so many elements of what I am talking about took place that I think the result was completely consonant with the suggestions I have been making today.

Georgetown is highly decentralized, and executive vice presidents of law and medicine and the main campus are close to provosts in their own domains. In 1995, faculty on our main campus, consisting of the college of arts and sciences, the school of foreign service, and the business school, created a representative faculty governance body known as the main campus executive faculty, as a constructive means of relating to the executive vice president as well as a repudiation of the traditional faculty senate governance mechanism. After achieving recognition of their group playing a role in academic affairs on the main campus, one of their first projects was an analysis of the quality of intellectual life on the main campus. In particular, concerns that career advancement goals of our students all but obliterate taking seriously learning in the liberal arts tradition, a concern I suspect not unique to Georgetown. Their first move was, I thought, inspired: They formed a series of randomly selected focus groups of freshmen to find out where the students were. One of the findings from the focus groups was that entering students' impressions of Georgetown were, by and large, firmly fixed within their first 30 days on campus. So they developed a strategy to change students' initial impressions of Georgetown, prevailed on the dean of students to alter significantly the student orientation program, and convinced the president of the university to preside and participate in an opening day ceremony created out of their own imaginations.

The first formal activity of new Georgetown students this fall, after moving into their rooms, was participation in an academic convocation. The students moved to the gym across the campus, arriving at the door through a corridor of 175 applauding and welcoming faculty in full academic regalia who returned to school four or five days early. At the convocation, which was one of the most moving and dramatic academic events I have ever participated in, the students heard about the founding of the school, the civic republican and enlightenment ideas that informed the founder, the architectural, and other symbols of the institution. They were formally admitted into the academic community as they donned gowns and were told about the tradition of gowns and symbolism of the hoods they would receive at graduation. The president gave a warm and rousing speech on the significance and meaning of the collegiate experience. The students took an oath to uphold the honor code and help their fellow students in need.

The convocation was a stunning success. The following day scores of individual faculty led discussion seminars on some text, film, or poetry, and they reported phenomenal enthusiasm and participation by the entering students. Of course, the challenging work of the executive faculty on strengthening the intellectual dimension of the Georgetown educational experience has just begun, but it began well. And there were some unexpected by-products. Our administrative services director had been trying for years without success to change the move-in day for freshmen because the traffic snarl paralyzed the medical center and the university on a weekday. The faculty wanted a Sunday convocation and so move-in day changed to Saturday and was the smoothest in memory. The convocation was a hit with the parents because it gave dignity and closure to that murky, awkward, indeterminate, and sometimes difficult time of taking and leaving a child at college. Parents were thrilled to attend the formal investiture into the academic community. We were asked repeatedly how many years we had been doing this. Plans are already underway on how to improve next year's convocation; one suggestion was that we should put pledge cards at each parent's seat.

The convocation was the most significant morale builder for our main campus faculty in recent times. It was created, directed, produced, and planned in minute detail by an associate professor of English and an associate professor of business. They helped draft the president's speech, and they edited everyone else's speeches. The success of this experiment derived from a passionate and talented faculty leadership that mobilized a combination of faculty support, a trusting and cooperative administration, a joint determination to create an event to deal with a problem that undermined the integrity of what the institution sees as its mission, and the recognition of the importance of assuring a strong affective dimension in the overall strategy. I offer this example not as a significant success story, but to underscore the simple point that even a small milestone of progress like this illustrates the importance of a number of the issues I've raised about criteria for evaluating and guiding innovation and change in American higher education.

SUMMARY

My point is simply that actions or initiatives captured by technological metaphors like reengineering, quality management, right-sizing, and simulation need to be conceived of in the context of our larger purpose, which is to write the biography or story of the future of our institution and the way our institution must change. And if we are going to be realistic about the story of change, let me summarize:

1) It's about people's motivations and strategizing to influence them.

2) There is no formula, nor for that matter, if you think my example from Georgetown is relevant, does it even need to be written down—the story is uniquely yours, whether of success or failure.

3) Sorting the relevant from the irrelevant, the critical from the trivial is a vital set of choices; fundamental values, or identifying the character of the place is the basic framework of the story.

4) Context is critical. The institutional story must account for the larger social and more immediate competitive environments in which choices are made.

5) Be self-conscious about who are the authors of the story and who are the major players and actors in it.

6) Institutions like universities should never underestimate the importance of emotion and attachment and sense of loyalty and dedication it engenders.

7) Innovation needs to be placed in the larger history of the institution.

8) The framework of this story is critical. How will innovation affect the sense of the whole institution, if at all?

9) Writing the story forces us to extend and project our values, our traditions, our leadership, our institutional style, and politics into a vision, a sense of what we want to be.

ENDNOTES

1) This paragraph is taken from Kelly, M. J. (1996). Lives in the law: Larger dimensions of professional responsibility. *Social Responsibility: Business, Journalism, Law, Medicine, 22,* 33.

2) See also Clark, B. R. (1972). The organization saga in higher education. *Administrative Science Quarterly, 17,* 178.

3) For a fine description of the "expanding perimeters," the way in which the expansion of energy in the university flows to perimeters, see Zemsky, R., & Massy, W. (1995, November/December). Toward an understanding of our current predicaments. *Change.*

REFERENCES

Clark, B. R. (1972). The organization saga in higher education. *Administrative Science Quarterly, 17,* 178.

Clark, B. R. (1971). Belief and loyalty in college organization. *Journal of Higher Education, 42,* 499.

Clark, B. R. (1970). *The distinctive college: Antioch, Reed, and Swarthmore.* Chicago, IL: Aldine.

Collins, J. C., & Porras, J. I. (1996, September-October). Building your company's vision. *Harvard Business Review, 65.*

Collins, J. C., & Porras, J. I. (1994). *Built to last: Successful habits of visionary companies.* New York, NY: HarperBusiness.

Collins, J. C., & Porras, J. I. (1991, Fall). Organizational vision and visionary organizations. *California Management Review, 30.*

Kelly, M. J. (1994). *Lives of lawyers.* Ann Arbor, MI: University of Michigan.

Kronman, A. (1987). Living the law. *University of Chicago Law Review, 54,* 854-855.

Selznick, P. (1957). *Leadership in administration.* Evanston, IL: Row, Peterson.

Taylor, C. (1991). *The ethics of authenticity.* Cambridge, MA: Harvard University Press.

Campus-Wide Approach to Systems Planning

Frederick A. Rogers

igher education is at a threshold. Resources are constrained, expectations are rising, and new forms of competition are arising in the private sector. New technologies have the potential to improve management and change the way people learn. They allow us to take advantage of efficiencies to pursue new opportunities that are vital to our mission of teaching, research, and public service. Yet, to some, the concept of managing a university is antithetical to the highly valued notion of academic freedom. Even as universities are under pressure to do more with less, to be more accountable to research sponsors and donors, and to respond to more student needs with smaller increases in tuition, some argue that business practices have no place in an academic setting. Universities are called upon to cut their overhead and reduce unneeded administrative costs, but expect to do so without investments or disruptions to established practices and prerogatives.

Many comprehensive universities are beginning to come to grips with the opportunities for significantly better management. In the name of autonomy and decentralization, universities have allowed duplicate and arcane practices to abound. Some of these are indeed part of the nature of academic freedom, such as multiple efforts in course and curriculum development or research design by individual faculty. Other practices are not, such as the independent student registration, accounting, and purchasing functions throughout the campus' departments. Initiating and succeeding at campus-wide change is not a common experience, especially at larger colleges and universities. How can we use the new-found motivations and opportunities to enable significant, successful change? What would constitute success?

CORNELL UNIVERSITY'S GOAL: BECOMING A BEST-MANAGED UNIVERSITY

At Cornell we are working to implement a model for business reengineering adapted to higher education. We seek to do this by building on the traditions of broad involvement, organizational autonomy, and diversity which characterize many research universities. We have dubbed this effort Making Cornell a Best-Managed University, or simply Project 2000. In particular, Project 2000 seeks to transform administrative support services through reengineering and implementing new administrative software systems in five key areas:

- Human resources/payroll

- Student administration

- Finance

- Sponsored programs

- Alumni affairs and development

The goal is to bring the advantage of the best management practices to bear, while emphasizing our mission and character as a university. This paper discusses our efforts to accomplish this in the administrative side of the university. A second set of efforts are underway to reorganize academic functions and departments, but that must be the subject of a second report at another time.

MEASURING SUCCESS

Many people and organizations are engaged in the pursuit of better ways of managing their operations. Whether we call it reengineering, business process improvement, restructuring, or downsizing, it is time for change on many campuses. We are under pressure to do more with less, and many of us feel the need to do something about reducing administrative costs. The hardest question is not "What we should do?"; it is "How do we do it successfully?" Any careful observer on a campus can identify ways in which administrative work and practice could be simplified and improved. But how does one get a large diverse organization such as a research university to change in a collective and directed fashion? Is such a change process antithetical to the nature of the institution?

At Cornell, we have tried to approach our goal of becoming a best-managed university by keeping in mind both the goal of better management and the goal of being an excellent university. We have started with several basic premises:

- Resources are tight and are going to be tighter.

- We need to reinvest in the academic program if we are to continue to be excellent.

- We can be more effective solving our infrastructure problems collectively than individually.

- We know more about how Cornell operates and how we would like it to operate than we know about how to design modern, efficient information systems.

- We are willing to invest several years of effort and resources in substantial improvement.

- We must see some benefits and improvements delivered along the way.

- When we finish, we want knowledge of our systems to be broadly resident at Cornell University.

- The campus broadly—not only the administrative units narrowly—should benefit from any such endeavor.

CORNELL UNIVERSITY'S EXPERIENCE IN THE FIRST YEAR

In "Why Transformation Efforts Fail," John Kotter (1995) suggests eight steps to transformation:

■ Establish a sense of urgency.

■ Form a powerful guiding coalition.

■ Create a vision.

■ Communicate the vision.

■ Empower others to act on the vision.

■ Plan for and create short-term wins.

■ Consolidate improvements and produce still more change.

■ Institutionalize new approaches.

I have chosen to use the taxonomy of Kotter's paper to illustrate what we are doing. It is important to remember that this is not the way we conceived of this effort. I find it a useful structure within which to describe and evaluate our efforts, but we did not have this road map in front of us as we began. And if we had, I am not sure we would have followed it. In a sense, we have had to find our own way; perhaps each institution must do the same. However, in looking back I think it is fair to say that these steps do represent essential markers on the road toward accomplishment of our goals. At some point we have to accomplish these things if we are to proceed. For that reason, it is useful to use this taxonomy retroactively to analyze what we have done.

Establishing a Sense of Urgency

If you don't have a sense of urgency, it is very hard to get started. The clear question is "Why bother?" At the outset, we had two hurdles to overcome: One was explaining why we should spend significant resources on a new endeavor, and the other was explaining why units of the university should give up their autonomy in any substantial way to do something collectively. Two elements helped us move from talking about the need to do something to actually doing it. The first was the realization that the good old days of growth were over and the second was the need to make better use of technology. In 1995 the Cornell trustees appointed Hunter Rawlings III as president of the university. In early discussions with Rawlings, it was clear that his priorities for academic initiatives and excellence could not all be financed from new revenue. Reducing our existing cost structure, especially in administrative overhead areas, would be essential to his plan to move the university forward. As we talked further with deans, trustees, faculty, and staff across campus, we developed a crisp message focused on "Why change?" We drafted a one sentence mission statement for Project 2000 which embodied our goal of creating a best-managed university:

> Reengineer Cornell's management policies and practices to
> focus all human, financial, and capital resources on excelling
> at the core missions of education, research, and public service.

To answer why change is necessary now, we wanted to convey two themes. The following is a paraphrase of several presentations I made across campus to convey these central themes:

Cornell, like other universities, must change because of increased competition and reduced resources. Competition continues to increase for the best students, faculty, and staff. Competition for government and private support is also increasing. Our analysis of trends over the past 25 years tells us that future availability of resources from these sources will not allow "business as usual" approaches. Like most universities today, we have no choice but to become more efficient, and technology can help us gain both efficiency and service improvement.

These are the "good old days." Technology change will not slow down. We cannot stand still; we have to improve or deteriorate. We have more flexibility now than we will have in the future. If we do not do something about antiquated processes and systems now, we will find ourselves with fewer discretionary resources and even more catch-up to do. We will also become increasingly noncompetitive in the level of service we can provide.

Just telling people that things have got to change does not create a sense of urgency. They also need some data. Two graphs helped make the case very convincingly at Cornell. Figure 5.1 is my favorite graph.

It shows four sources of revenue for Cornell displayed in 1970-71 dollars and tracked over 20 years. Looking at this graph creates a sense of urgency. Major revenue streams have stopped growing. State and federal appropriations remain unchanged, while gifts and grants, which experienced a growth phase through the mid-1980s, have also gone flat. Only tuition has continued to grow, and no one believes it can sustain that growth rate.

FIGURE 5.1

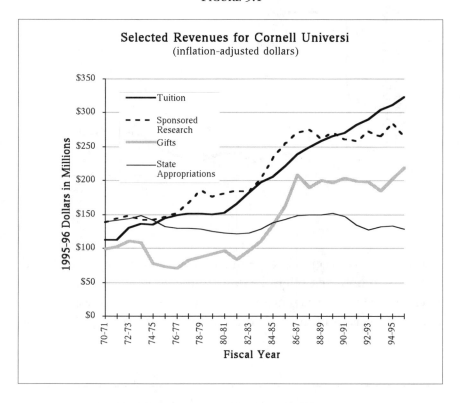

In fact, when we look more closely at tuition, we see that the level of tuition is a real issue for many, if not most, of our students. The second chart we have used extensively (Figure 5.2) is one which shows the relationship between tuition and family income. Increasing tuition year after year is not an alternative. Faced with declining revenues, we must spend less money, or get more for the money we spend.

FIGURE 5.2

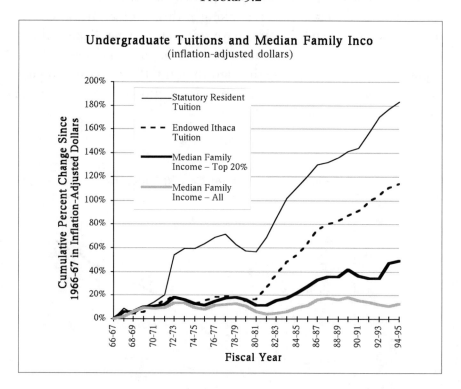

People may accept that we must spend less money, but they do not relate to how that might be done until we show some examples of where we are not very efficient. In the summer of 1994, we looked at some processes in human resources to find out just how efficient we are (see Table 5.1).

TABLE 5.1

Creating a new position requires	Filling that position requires
6 forms	10 forms
6 systems	8+ systems
13 redundant filings	7 redundant filings
35 hand-offs	46 hand-offs
Handling time of 8 to 58 hours	Handling time of 4 to 5 hours
Cycle time of 10 days to 5 months	Cycle time of 10 to 25 days

Clearly there is potential to take costs and non-value-added work out of these processes.

This is the sense of urgency we have tried to communicate across campus. As one of the deans said, "No one else will do this—it is our imperative and responsibility. We do not have much time and if the campus is ready it is our obligation to try."

Forming a Powerful Guiding Coalition

The problems of a large university cannot be solved by one administrator in a centralized project like Project 2000. These are fundamental problems that require involvement from people in administration at all levels of the university. We could not have undertaken a project of this scope without the unqualified support of the president and the provost, and we have enjoyed that support as we continue. The president expresses our goals in talks with trustees, faculty, and staff; and the provost is actively involved in policy decisions and communication. Moreover, the provost has let all deans, faculty, and staff know that he and the senior vice president are in this together as a team and that we all seek the same objective: a better university.

We have formed coalitions of two natures to support Project 2000: those whose support is important if we are to succeed and those who possess the knowledge and motivation to do the work that needs to be done. Taking a cue from the earlier quality council, we have engaged the provost, deans, and senior administrators in an overall board of directors role to enable the solutions we need to implement. At the onset skepticism was high, and bringing the skeptics into a high-level council gave them a place to express skepticism and receive information that will decrease that skepticism. It also provided focus and motivation to the project leadership.

As we began the project, we used the group of administrative vice presidents, meeting to determine systems policy, as our basic policy oversight group. We put the first tough question—whether to buy all of our systems from PeopleSoft—to this group. We brought this group tough questions of changing our implementation partner and hiring a dedicated project manager. And it was to this group that we put the issue of budget choices. All of our resources invested in new systems and reengineering would mean very little could be invested in changes to existing systems and practices in the interim, which could last for up to three years. It is a real testament to the individuals and to Cornell that this group has stayed together and supported each other, even when we have been unable to reach full consensus and when choices have clearly differentiated outcomes for members of the group. Their willingness always to seek the best collective outcome for the university has been a key element in our project's success.

As we organized the project, we filled key management positions with high-level managers from the five core areas and from academic and administrative units across campus. A coalition between the central administration and colleges and units is essential for this project to be a campus-wide transformation. The level of people required to work on the project is very high, because reengineering requires both a broad view of the university and in-depth knowledge of particular areas. This is not the kind of project that can be done by people who are dispensable in their functional area. Taking away the best people in an area for over a year to work on a project that benefits the whole university causes sacrifice in already short-staffed areas, yet the sacrifice is unavoidable. The broad coalition of deans, vice presidents, and others around campus has been essential in the recruitment of campus talent to this effort.

Creating a Vision

Our one sentence mission is "Project 2000, creating a best-managed university—reengineer Cornell's management policies and practices to focus all human, financial, and capital resources on excelling at the core missions of education, research, and public service." At a retreat of administrators and faculty in December 1995, we asked the group to imagine what Cornell would be like in the year 2001 if we were successful with our project. They envisioned a Cornell in 2001 where:

- We dedicate a greater proportion of resources to teaching, research, and public service activities.

- We hold the increase in the cost of attending Cornell close to inflation.

- We have the highest student satisfaction rating for administrative services among Consortium for Financing Higher Education (COFHE) institutions.

- We have fewer employees, who will be better compensated.

- We spend more time solving problems and less time processing transactions.

- We spend less money on administration.

In 1993 and 1994 Cornell undertook an extensive strategic planning effort, as the result of an accreditation report which recommended more attention to strategic planning. In a strategic planning report issued in 1994, a group was tasked to look at stewardship issues. To paraphrase the group's report: "If we really want to change the way we work, we have to change the organizational structures as well, and we have to enable that with technology." We had built our own administrative systems at Cornell, and each core administrative area had made independent decisions about requirements and design. While we had some success in creating tools for students to obtain access to their grades and change their addresses and those tools had relieved students of long waits in line, we still had no integrated system for managing student registration, financial aid, and billing. Our payroll system was woefully inadequate and would be very expensive to update to handle the Year 2000. Systems to meet the business needs of the finance, sponsored programs, and alumni areas did not exist and would be prohibitively expensive to develop and maintain. We had some success in creating tools for students to obtain access to their grades and change their addresses and those tools had relieved students of long waits in line.

Each major area of the university understood that technology could help them be more efficient and provide better service. But everyone wanted to do their own thing. The student administration area wanted to develop its own system. Human resources wanted to buy PeopleSoft's HR/payroll system. The financial area did not even want to think about a new system now, but meanwhile several colleges were implementing Hyperion. Sponsored programs proposed working with American Management Systems (AMS) to develop a system, and alumni affairs and development wanted the Business Systems Resources (BSR) system.

The new vice president for technology and I worked together very closely in 1994 and 1995 to develop a strategy for technology at Cornell. In the fall of 1994, we spoke to a group of administrators and technical people about our vision of how the world would be if we really got technology right. Out of this discussion came a single-page written summary for discussion. We emphasized that we had an opportunity to choose a solution that could grow to benefit the whole institution. In the process of discussing this technology vision and strategy, the group of administrative vice presidents identified three key building blocks of a transformational project:

- We agreed upon a technical vision for what Cornell administrative systems must do and facilitate as an outcome.

- We agreed that we would buy, not build, systems.

- We agreed to start with an initiative to identify a vendor to supply an human resource system.

The technology vision, which helped us immeasurably in deciding on a strategy, can be distilled to three bullets:

- Core technologies will be available and in common use.

- Information interdependencies will be widely understood and accepted.

- Customers will experience fully informed responses and services.

It became clear that although this was a technology vision, it had profound impact on the quality of administrative services at Cornell. As just one example, walking around campus an observer would find that every department has invented its own system and ways of dealing with administration of the institution. People in each department learn how the system works from their predecessors or their neighbors. This model leads to two fundamental problems. First, if someone is hired into an academic department as an administrator, what they learn about how to deal with graduate student appointments, for example, has almost no transferability to working with budgets, research grants, or purchasing. There are literally different technologies, different computers, and different definitions. Centrally, Cornell organizes around functions, and within a function, everything feels somewhat uniform. But at the unit level, one person has to deal with all the functions, and they are not the least bit uniform. A second problem is that if someone gets a new job in a different department, they will find that most of what they learned in the first department has very little bearing on their job in the new department. Having no transferability of skills and no uniformity in training is really costly. Our envisioned solution to these problems is to have more or less the same way of doing things from one unit to the next, so the institution can train people and they can move around more easily from task to task and from unit to unit.

I cannot stress enough the power of a succinctly stated, shared vision. Our technology vision deliberations helped us in making decisions. Those three bullets were the result of six months of debate and discussion, but at the end of that discussion, everyone involved had a clear idea of our common intention. Over the next six months we thoroughly examined three strategies: a "best of breed" approach, a trial relationship with a vendor for one system, and a commitment to one proven vendor to jointly develop all of our core systems. After extensive investigation and analysis, we prepared to move ahead with the third strategy: replacing all of our core systems with a common technology purchased from one vendor and implemented in a common systems architecture. Without a vision to test alternatives against, we might still be trying to make a decision. It has continued to add value as we approach issues of process reengineering and organizational structure. We all do better if we have some common principles to reference in these hard decisions.

Communicating the Vision

I have already talked about the role of communication in creating a sense of urgency. Once we had a vision for the project, I incorporated it into talks across campus. I have given over 25 presentations to a variety of staff and faculty groups, and that probably is not enough.

We need to keep finding new ways to explain to people what this project will do for them and for the institution. We found that we cannot communicate enough and that there is no single best way to communicate. Different people prefer getting information through different media. So we have a web page, and we publish a newsletter. We send information to electronic mail lists, and we write articles in campus newspapers. Realizing that getting out and talking to people about what we mean by this vision is even more important than writing about it, we talk to groups, large and small.

It is important for the people working on Project 2000 to keep in mind the principles guiding their work. We have given nearly 100 people working on teams a pinup list to keep above their desks reminding them of some basic principles:

- Standardize practices, don't customize software

- Eliminate unnecessary work

- Reduce authorizations, expand access

- Distribute work, aggregate information

- Follow the "rules of one":
     Data entered once at the source
     Data stored and defined once
     Transactions approved once

Communication has been a real learning process. We had a strategy. We thought we had choreographed a great beginning with a piece in a campus paper with the headline "The president unveils Project 2000—strategy to change the university." We were getting the message out.

The president is behind it; the provost is behind it; we are trying to create a best-managed university. We've signed a contract with PeopleSoft, and we're on our way.

The problem is, messages are not always interpreted the way we would like them to be. The day after our campus announcement, the local Ithaca newspaper picked up the story and ran it with the headline "CU computer upgrade to eliminate jobs."

One of the services we plan to improve, and one we thought faculty would find exciting, is student advising. After an article in the campus newspaper on our plans in that area, we got a letter from a faculty member with this perspective: "I think this is a university administrator's fantasy. Perhaps someday we'll never have to see students. Faculty could stay in their private offices, which is where they really want to be anyway, and instead of dealing with students they could get to know their network IDs."

And a graduate student who looked at our web pages wrote us email starting off, "I like this whole idea of bureaucracy thinking it can trim itself down. I can just picture the meeting. 'Yes, today Johnson and myself will be eliminating our positions. Good-bye!' The administrative red tape here could wrap around Mars seven times and then dangle its way back to earth."

Although those perspectives may seem harsh, we are glad people are sharing them. We have incorporated the comments on red tape into our communications, explaining that we are fighting a war against Big Red Tape. In fact, because Cornell's athletic teams are known as "The Big Red," we have adopted the notion of fighting Big Red Tape and have put out flyers and banners with this slogan. We continue to communicate as often and in as many media as we possible can, with a strategy of answering the questions that arise at any particular time.

One example of the need for communication was the fall forum for staff concerned about the impacts of Project 2000. The employee assembly of Cornell asked the administration if we would host an open meeting with concerned staff to discuss the issues of job security, training, and impact of the project. We imagined this would be expanded from their normal lunch meetings with administrators where about 20 people attend to something maybe as large as 100. By the time the meeting was held, it had moved to our large concert hall and was attended by over 1,200 individuals. The panel discussion and question and answer period went on for an hour, after the formal presentations. While most of the information conveyed in this forum was not new, for many of the staff it was the first time they had ever met face-to-face with the president, provost, and others to discuss such issues. Everyone seemed to feel this was helpful, and we are planning to do it again this fall.

Empowering Others to Act on the Vision

One of my principal objectives as an administrator is to remove obstacles that hamper others acting on the vision. Once we had organized and staffed project teams, engaged an external consultant, done some preliminary planning, communicated our vision across campus, and started in earnest looking at the PeopleSoft HR/payroll project, we thought it was time to take stock. Were we really succeeding, or were structures, cultures, and attitudes working against us?

We found several issues working against us:

- Project organization

- Methodology and expertise

- Structural opportunities

- Objectives and measurements

- Project focus

- Project savings

In the summer of 1996, I took this list of issues and proposed solutions to the assembled deans and executive staff of the university. We discussed their perceptions of what was working and what was not and our project data of our own analysis. Everyone was appreciative of a frank and direct assessment. We collectively decided to act on these issues and promised to revisit them during the coming academic year. The following is a summary of four of these issues and how we addressed them.

Project organization. We had created a project structure that was managed by a committee. The managers of ten project teams met weekly in a meeting that was cochaired by a technical director and a reengineering director. No one was sure who was in charge: Sufficient accountability and authority did not exist within the project. This state had resulted from our attempts to balance autonomy and share responsibility. It seemed natural not to demote or promote any one colleague too much in the collaborative effort in which we were engaged. But it became clear that this model would not bring us the success we desired. We spent another three months debating how to proceed, what type of project manager was appropriate, and interviewing several candidates. In the end, the project executives agreed to hire a senior, experienced project director who had led other institutions through transformation projects. We gave the project director the authority and an incentive structure necessary to guide the project.

Methodology and expertise. There was no single project methodology which brought together all the components of a transformation project of this complexity. The project leadership void had created a multiplicity of approaches on each team. Moreover, our implementation partner was not able to provide an overall project plan that could be endorsed by all parties. This resulted in project teams creating their own approaches, as well as campus partners not understanding how issues were to be discussed and resolved. Additionally, we did not have sufficient PeopleSoft expertise on campus to guide us through the technical and functional impact of a PeopleSoft implementation. We reconsidered our implementation consulting relationship and decided to hire Andersen Consulting as an implementation partner. Again, this change required several months of discussion among the project leadership, careful negotiations with our previous partner and with Andersen, and then a significant time commitment to bring the new consultant up to speed. The test we applied was the same: Will our present course bring us success? If not, what must we do to achieve our goals? We have found that Andersen has a strong, detailed, and balanced methodology, and superior PeopleSoft expertise and confidence and momentum have been restored in the project.

Objectives and measurements. While we had discussed the overall project mission and goals, confusion remained as to what the specific objectives of the project were. We charged a team of college faculty and administrators to define as specifically as possible the objectives they wished to use to measure our success. This team, called TEAM^2 (Team for Evaluation and Measurement), developed the following objectives:

■ Increase satisfaction of faculty, students, staff, and other clients by providing the training, tools, and information they need to do their work better, and by improving the quality and effectiveness of information and administrative services.

■ Enhance the productivity, competence, and career satisfaction of administrative staff by eliminating work that adds no value and providing them with training, tools, and information to enable them to maximize their capabilities.

■ Reduce administrative costs and allow reinvestment in academic priorities by redesigning administrative policies, structures, and processes and making better use of advanced technologies and information systems to enhance efficiency and effectiveness.

Since we are working on an aggressive schedule to finish the bulk of the system implementation by the year 2000, we are trying to balance the time necessary to measure the current situation against the need to move on.

Project focus. The project has been perceived as a technology implementation project. This is not surprising, considering that it involves major technology replacement and has resulted in major decisions about technology strategies. However, a strictly technical focus will not motivate the broad representation needed to carry out a true transformation and works against meeting all of the project objectives. With the advent of the project director we reorganized the existing teams and created a separate reengineering team, charged with supporting the implementation teams in activities such as process mapping and executive sponsorship. Our communications strategy has changed to reflect a balanced approach, describing the project as an initiative to change:

■ Structure, organization, people

■ Process

■ Technology

Strong leadership of the reengineering effort has resulted in much more uniform attention to the reengineering aspects of the project. Executive sponsor groups are actively engaged in determining what processes are most critical, what policies need changing, and what the limitations are. As a result, the perceived focus is now more evenly balanced on both process change and technology implementation.

The point of these examples is to show that no matter how well conceived a project is at the outset, it is important to reevaluate regularly and adapt to developing circumstances and needs. None of these changes were easy, nor were they immediately accepted. However, in each case the process of identifying the need for the change, discussing the options, and ultimately forcing ourselves to make a selection and move on was healthy and enabling.

Plan for and create short-term wins. People need to see results. Showing them a timeline that says we'll have a new financial system in 1999 does not inspire the confidence that seeing and using just one small piece of new technology inspires. The PeopleSoft systems, which were to be finished in 1998 at the earliest, are most apt to be used by a small number of people dedicated to a specific function. The benefit that comes through better access to information will be provided through what we are calling "accessory technologies," such as data warehouses and reports, web access, and workflow technologies.

Beginning with an accounting data warehouse in January 1998, we introduced short-term wins in each of the core areas:

- HR/payroll: electronic time collection and a new employee data warehouse

- Student administration: enhancement to the current student self-serve system (Just the Facts) and a new student data warehouse.

- Finance: nearly 100 people have been trained in the use of the new accounting data warehouse.

- Sponsored programs: web-based services for principal investigators and a data warehouse for research accounting.

- Alumni affairs and development: enhanced special prospect information.

The benefit of short-term wins is not only that people will see some results, but also that they will begin to experience the benefits of technology and develop skills in its use as the project progresses.

MOVING PERSISTENTLY BEYOND THE YEAR 2000

Project 2000 is at a point where we can only evaluate it with regard to six of Kotter's eight steps. As we move into implementation, we are keeping the last two in mind:

- Consolidate improvements and produce still more change. While short-term wins are important, the long-term project takes staying power. Implementing technology will require months of hard work, but adopting new processes and restructuring the way we provide administrative services will require a willingness to change that will not come easily. We must keep the vision in mind and persist, even when we think we've already produced incredible improvement. Each improvement becomes the basis for further change.

- Institutionalize new approaches. We will know we are successful when the changes we are planning now become the way we do things at Cornell. Solving the technology problems and avoiding computer malfunctions in the year 2000 will be easy compared to the education and communication we will undertake to make sure every person involved in providing or using administrative services at Cornell understands and believes in the new processes and systems we are using in the year 2000.

The path of transformation is not smooth, and Project 2000 at Cornell is no exception. We have thought and rethought, discussed and debated, communicated and listened. Taking stock of the project and making some dramatic changes was viewed by skeptics and cynics as a sign that we are very serious about achieving our objectives. To those who look at timelines, we may seem to be slipping, but our progress at this point cannot be measured on a calendar. Much of the initial work has been in gaining understanding, acceptance, and support. As we move into the implementation phase of the project, we will see how much the initial investment in creating a sense of urgency and a vision and communicating has paid off.

Faced with a project of this scope, it is tempting to wonder if we have committed ourselves to a larger goal than we need to. We believe we have no choice. The difficult times now facing higher education administrators, faculty, and students can be seen as adversity or opportunity. If seen as the latter, there is reason to believe that great strides can be made in making the university a more effective and service-oriented environment, without great increases in resources.

The main lesson of our experiences so far at Cornell is this: There is more to be gained from doing the next thing right than from trying to do everything right at the outset. In discussing this with a number of people, I have often used the metaphor of this effort being like a crusade. It is important to motivate everyone enough to support the cause and be willing to leave on such a journey. But it is so long, and so impossible to foresee all that will be necessary, that we must trust to our ability to adapt and "live off the land" as we go for our ultimate success. We cannot begin with every possible problem solved and every contingency covered in our initial planning. But how do we balance planning and organizing up front with action? Isn't this always the tough choice? The old joke that "Ready, Aim, Fire" is translated on campuses to "Ready, Ready, Ready" has the opposite problem when it becomes "Fire, Ready, Aim." Maybe it becomes more like what usually happens in practice anyway: "Ready, Aim, Fire, Aim, Fire, Aim, Fire, Ready." I have ended many of my talks around campus with the following statement, which is becoming true at Cornell: "Together we are capable of doing more than we imagine."

For all of the people who read the management texts and wonder how their organization can ever follow all of those steps and processes, given that they cannot even agree on the basic objectives, I want to provide some comfort. If you find anything to agree on, start there. We are now doing more than we could have imagined or been willing to undertake at the outset. And it is only possible because of three things: a willingness to start, a willingness to adapt and reevaluate, and a willingness to support each other even when we were uncertain. For these reasons I am confident that Cornell will succeed and that others can too.

REFERENCES

Kotter, J. (1995, March-April). Why transformation efforts fail. *Harvard Business Review.*

6

Manic Over Measures:
Measuring, Evaluating, and Communicating Administrative Performance in Higher Education

Richard N. Katz

Count on what is countable;
measure what is measurable;
and what is not measurable, make measurable.

Galileo Gaililei

WHY MEASURE?

People like to measure. In any social setting, we are likely to hear: "I lost 4 pounds in the first week," or "My mutual fund earned 21% last year," or "Barry Bonds' 48 home runs at this stage of the season puts him on a pace to beat Babe Ruth's record!" Measures are a touchstone for many things. Used properly, measures can tell us where we've been, where we are, and where we are going. Measures can also inform us of how fast we are going, and in what direction we're heading.

Intelligent measures can guide our decisions: "A support structure of X strength cannot bear Y weight." Measures can be normative and can assist in planning: "I want to lose 20 pounds in two months. I have lost only five pounds in my first three weeks. I need to change my diet or exercise program [or my goal]." Measures can also be used to make meaningful comparisons: "It took me two hours to perform this task that took you only an hour."

Measures also are used to diagnose health or vitality. Macroeconomists measure the changes in prices in the market prices of goods over time, the rate of unemployment, and other indicators to determine the relative health of the economy and to formulate monetary or fiscal policy. Investors study corporate earnings, debt, market share, cashflow, and other factors to inform investment decisions. Physicians measure and monitor heart rates, blood pressure, body weight, cholesterol levels, and other aspects of body function and chemistry to assess risk and to suggest interventions.

Most importantly, when used statistically, measures can help us form intelligent assumptions about the future. The magic of measures is contextual. Financial data, without an underlying financial model, is no more or no less than a data point. To know one's blood pressure, without the context of the patient's age or the reservoir of historical data correlating such data to the risk of heart disease, is of no value. Similarly, knowing that the fuel gauge reads full is an insufficient indicator of your car's tripworthiness. Conversely, good measurement information set in a context-normative (against goals), comparative (against meaningful exemplars), or longitudinal can be powerful and rewarding in personal, managerial, and governance contexts.

If measures are good, but insufficient, what is better is a "measurement system." Effective measurement systems implicitly and explicitly guide our choices. As consumers, many of us depend on *Consumer Reports* to evaluate an appliance's reliability, depreciation rate, owner satisfaction, or other attributes of quality. The measurement system of *Consumer Reports* exhibits in a simple fashion some of the major elements of a powerful measurement system:

1) It measures quality using multiple variables.

2) It incorporates quantitative and qualitative measures.

3) It makes intelligent comparisons.

4) It incorporates longitudinal information.

5) It identifies "best of class" (best buys).

6) It is intuitively sensible and easy to understand.

Just as people like measures, people also like measurement systems. Consciously or unconsciously, most of us know that ice cream has more calories from fat than do carrots or celery. Each of us walks around with arcane data based on old measures that we process through implicit measurement systems in order to derive some of our rational decisions (e. g., "I don't think I'll eat that ice cream cone," or "I think I'll buy the Honda.").

SO WHAT'S THE PROBLEM?

If we can agree that measurement is an activity that makes sense and is perhaps intuitively accessible to *homo universitadas,* why are many of us "manic over measures"?[1] At least four major factors contribute to higher education's current preoccupation with measurement. The factors are related to budget, governance, management, and culture. The first, and most obvious, factor is the changed external climate facing the industry. The late 1980s and early 1990s were characterized by significant declines in revenue growth across most sectors of the industry. A "baby bust" of college-eligible students during this period sharpened competition within the independent college segment, while increasing pressures to balance state and federal budgets reduced the flow of these funds into the public university sectors. These pressures on revenues have led in the short-term to widespread tuition and fee increases, to significant increases in institutionally based financial aid, and to an increasing focus of attention on institutional costs, particularly, the costs of "administration." The higher education price index (HEPI), the dominant market basket index of college and university tuition prices, has long exceeded the consumer price index, that proxy of other goods and services available in the economy. The disparity in this price rise is not a factor of growth, so much as it is an indicator of higher education's inability to rein in costs (Massy & Zemsky, 1990). The revenue pressures facing institutions, the need to combat a growing credibility problem with key stakeholders, the growing concern over tuition discounting, and the increasing resolve of many trustees and presidents to slow tuition increases create the need for presidents and trustees to manage more closely and understand better their institutions' "business," driving, in turn, an enhanced interest in measures, benchmarking, and cost studies.

What's worse is the fact that the consuming and voting public has become aware of fast-rising higher education prices and has concluded, right or wrong, that such price escalation must be due to inefficient management. In this vein, the second major driver of the current mania for measures is the changing public perception of U.S. higher education. The end of the Second World War, the success of the Manhattan Project, and the passage of the G. I. Bill of Rights ushered in a period of unprecedented government support of U.S. higher education. Higher education—as a public value—moved from being considered the exclusive domain of the social, economic, and gender elite to being viewed as a public good. A college education was viewed as the universal vehicle for individual citizenship and economic advancement, and university-based research was viewed as the engine for the U.S. domination of global scientific and economic development. U.S. colleges and universities, particularly research universities, enjoyed unprecedented prosperity in the 1950s and 1960s under the impetus of a host of state and federal programs designed to lower the barriers to economic barriers to enrollment and others to finance basic research.

As concerns about government deficits and U.S. economic competitiveness have grown, important attitudal shifts among key higher educational stakeholder groups such as governments, business, parents, and students themselves have occurred. The essence of this shift is one away from the concept of a higher education as a public good or entitlement, to a concept of a postsecondary education as a public investment. This shift manifests itself in a variety of ways. First, and perhaps most powerful, are the sharpening cries for accountability and administrative efficiency in public higher education (see Table 6.1).

TABLE 6.1

High Priority Issues by Viewpoint
(in percentages)

	Governor	Legislators	Systems	Chancellors
Administrative Bloat	24.5	32.1	11.3	7.5
Teaching Load	20.8	35.8	30.2	26.4
Accountability	58.5	71.7	43.7	35.8
Graduation Rates	18.9	37.7	39.6	54.7
Program Duplication	34.0	35.8	26.4	7.5
Minority Retention	9.4	9.4	30.2	50.9

(Source: *Report of the States,* (1995, September). Washington, DC: American Association of State Colleges and Universities, 1.)

Accountability, in particular, is a problematic concept that means different things to different people. At the core, however, is the suggestion that something is "rotten in Denmark," as regards to the use of public funds. The call for increased accountability is the clear signal of a shift from a belief that faculty and administrators are faithful stewards of our young people's and nation's future, to a belief that we are "pigs at the public trough," who—like many others—must be overseen and regulated if we are to make wise use of public funds. While this language is perhaps too colorful, it seems reasonable to be argued that a part of the mania for measurement, including pressures to change the Financial Accounting Standards Board (FASB) and Government Accounting Standards Board (GASB) reporting models, derive from the enhanced public desire for familiar corporate-style accountabilities, like return on investment. The shift in public beliefs about the costs and value of a higher education are also reflected in the increased popularity of the popular press-based efforts to rank colleges and universities. There is a *Consumer Reports*-ization of the complex and diverse missions of U.S. colleges and universities that is a powerful indicator of the new awareness of postsecondary education as a consumer good and an equally strong indicator of a lack public confidence in higher education's ability to either convey our own performance in meaningful terms, or to align our priorities with broad public sentiment. Most major research universities dread the annual *Business Week, Money,* and other popular ranking issues, spend considerable hours wringing hands in despair of the analytical poverty of such studies, and trumpet instead the qualititative and inward-looking rankings of such esteemed groups as the National Research Council (when such surveys demonstrate a preference for our institutions!). Right or wrong, the mania over measures is being driven externally in part.

A third impetus for the current fascination with measurement is managerial and derives in large measure from both the economic and accountability pressures described. In recognition of attenuating revenue streams, of some of the inherent managerial shortcomings of the shared governance model, of the growing potential posed by networked information resources, and of the year 2000 risks posed by their aging information infrastructures, many institutions are engaged in unprecedented activity designed to reformulate their fundamental management models and business processes.

Whether described as reengineering, reinvention, transformation, renewal, or in some other way, many U.S. colleges and universities are engaged in projects of huge scope that will alter the ways in which they conduct business. Many of these change initiatives are intrinsically measurement intensive. Responsibility Center Management (RCM), for example, seeks to align institutional and individual economic behavior by placing the responsibility for campus economic performance with key institutional subunits: schools, colleges, auxiliaries, etc. The effectiveness of this management model depends on the timely and meaningful flow of revenue and expense information, the identification and allocation of institutional and subunit costs, and hence, measures and a measurement system. Other efforts depend less directly on measurement, but can and should be discharged in close conjunction with new measurement activity. Process reengineering, for example, is premised on the belief that identifying and managing the core "horizontal" processes of a campus (acquiring goods, enrolling students, acquiring grants, etc.) makes it possible to improve the performance of such processes and to reduce their costs.

Major research universities and others are placing large bets on the promise of reengineering, but few can describe such attributes of processes as "What does it cost to purchase a low-value good?" or "How long does it take to create, classify, recruit, and fill a staff position?" Having persuaded their presidents and trustees to invest tens of millions of dollars to reengineer core processes, it seems reasonable to expect that someone, someday will seek a more-than-anecdotal accounting of improvements in service quality and cost in the wake of these investments. Manic over measures!

The fourth, and perhaps most problematic source of higher education's current preoccupation and difficulty with measurement is university culture. If the popular or academic characterization of universities as adhocracies (Cohen & March, 1974), or as "amiable, anarchic, self-correcting collectives of scholars with a small contingent of dignified caretakers at the unavoidable business edge" (Keller, 1983) no longer either conforms to the realities of the modern multiversity or at least to the changing public expectations of colleges and universities, the complexity of the higher education mission and the pervasiveness of essential academic values and norms make agreement on specific measures very difficult. Massy and Zemsky (1990) make the compelling case regarding the diffusion of academic culture, values, and expectations within the administrative cadre of the academy. Chief among these values, vis-à-vis measurement, are 1) an abiding belief in the organizational uniqueness of colleges and universities, 2) a deep distrust of solutions originating in industry, 3) a reverence for analytical rigor and method, 4) and a concomitant love of accuracy and truth (Weik, 1984). If the perhaps naive mantra of industry is "if it can't be measured, it can't be managed," the equally naive myth of higher education is "bright people given plentiful (or unlimited) resources and dignified caretaking (not management) will consistently deliver great ... [scholarship, education ...]."

Whether or not the academic confidence in infinite resources, intelligence, and benign management is ideologically sustainable, it is clearly unsustainable in light of current economic and political realities. However, until faculty and staff accept these changed circumstances and conclude that the issue is not whether to measure, but whose measures will shape the institution (the academy's, the state government's, *Money* magazine's, the governing board's) selling measures and measurement systems on campus will be tough sledding.

As regards the academic culture of accuracy, this too places institutional measurement initiatives in jeopardy. The process of measurement for managerial and governance purposes is inherently heuristic and partially political. In most cases, the results of managerial measurement activity are "good enough for horseshoes" kinds of results, as such information is used to answer simple questions such as "Are we doing better or worse than before?" or "Are we more or less expensive than they are?" Methodological consistency, not infinitesimal accuracy, is the holy grail of measurement in the managerial and governance contexts. Of course, the relative importance of consistency over accuracy is in direct conflict with key academic values and nonacademic values held by administrators such as accountants or institutional researchers. The result of these culture conflicts is predictable: Measures and measurement activity will be refuted and resisted from nearly all quarters of the campus owing to their inaccuracy, irrelevance, or intrusiveness. Endless debate over the validity of individual measures is likely to blunt the resolve of even the most committed supporter. The simple truth is: We all like to measure, and we all hate to be measured!

THE LATTICE, THE RATCHET, AND THE PERFORMANCE ARCHITECTURE

William Massy and Robert Zemsky (1990) described aspects of campus culture and financial structure that contribute to the industry's penchant to grow through accretion and to eschew the substitution of old programs when new programs are conceived. The administrative lattice in many ways crystallizes around a business architecture that, at its core, is cost-additive and begs for reinvention. This architecture equates administrative performance with rule compliance.

The compliance-based performance architecture prevalent on college and university campuses is not antithetical to measurement and related concepts of statistical quality control, but operates from a different premise. The compliance-based performance architecture is premised on the belief that controlling procedures and following the rules either ensures, or is at least a surrogate for, good management and good results.

The administrative focus on procedural compliance reflects, in part, the difficulty of assessing the performance and outcomes of many campus administrative (and academic!) programs. It is easier to measure and evaluate whether or not the campus community has enrolled X students based on Y state funding, than to determine whether or not the campus delivers "quality" education. Similarly, it is easier to point to the success of a purchasing program that is free of adverse audit comments or disallowed federal purchases than it is to define and describe a good purchasing program. An outcome-based system or model of assessing performance of campus business functions or processes—like the assessment of faculty research—is complex, often qualitative, and usually depends on normative expectations (What should a good purchasing organization be doing?).

The weakness of the procedural control model lies in its premise that "the absence of negative findings is positive." In defense of the audit community, there was never an intention in audit theory to substitute the compliance review for sound management. In fact, good auditors will generally argue that good management practices generally cause good results, including compliance, and that compliance is only one indicator of a sound management system, not the management system itself. Notwithstanding good intentions, disproportionate campus administrative effort is directed at compliance with an ever-growing and self-perpetuating body of rules and regulations. Like Massy and Zemsky's ratchet, new rules rarely, if ever, replace old rules. The effects of the compliance-based performance architecture on administrative costs and quality are obvious. An audit of a campus administrative activity reveals a deficiency. In general, such deficiencies indicate one of a number of possible weaknesses:

- insufficient separation of duties

- inadequate management oversight

- no clear rule or procedures to address the specific weakness identified

In responding to such findings, campus management generally adds a new rule—failing typically to subtract an existing rule—and, in a paper-based procedural environment, amends campus forms to capture a certification that the new rule has been operationalized and complied with. To enhance management oversight, new lines are added to the signature block on the form to ensure that errant transactions are referred ever upward in the hope that someone in the management chain will spot—and prevent—the error from recurring (see Figure 6.1).

FIGURE 6.1

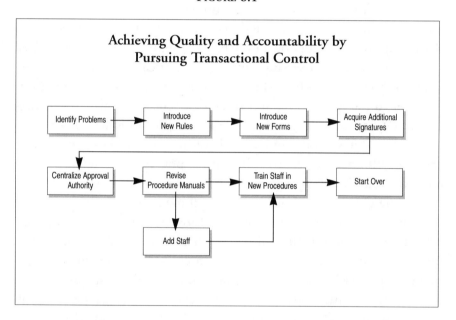

Achieving Quality and Accountability by Pursuing Transactional Control

Operationalizing this implicit management model, or performance architecture, produces a number of suboptimal and even dysfunctional effects. First, as the body of rules grows, the staff effort to assimilate, understand, and comply with the rules grows, resulting inevitably in either the need to add administrative staff or the growing risk of compliance failures as existing staff fail to keep up and as layers of rules become increasingly confounding. Increasing separation of duties, in organizations of small size, almost inevitably invites staff additions. The improvement of compliance through the upward referral of permissions and referrals results in the direction of hundreds of campus transactions up the administrative chain of command, reducing senior decision makers to approvers of transactions over which they exercise little substantive control and about which they understand little. Most important, a management system that is optimized for compliance seeks 100% compliance as an implicit goal. Such systems, and their implementing organizations, tend, over time, to become risk-averse naysayers, preferring the comfort of cut-and-dried (if unclear and irrational) rules, to the slippery slope of individual judgment and accountability. This is the dark side of the Weberian bureaucratic ideal!

You will note that an organization and management system that is optimized for compliance is not intrinsically preoccupied with other aspects and attributes of performance. If the rules confound the customer and business success depends on compliance with the rules, then campuses must be protected from rule-breaking customers (faculty and students).

Beginning around 1988, U.S. campuses began a flirtation with the quality movement, and TQM, CQI, and other buzzwords, acronyms, and concepts became a part of our vocabulary. Some of us achieved notable success incorporating these methodologies into our business practices, some of us decried the inapplicability of such corporate notions in the academy, and others of us quietly dispatched the concepts while embracing the buzzwords and rhetoric. The key concepts of the quality movement, those anchored in measurement of planned action and in statistical quality control, have not taken root on our campuses. In particular, the notions of the centrality of measurement to the management process and that of Pareto optimality (80-20 rule) have gained currency on few of our campuses. The role of measures is key to the establishment of a new performance architecture (see Figure 6.2).

FIGURE 6.2

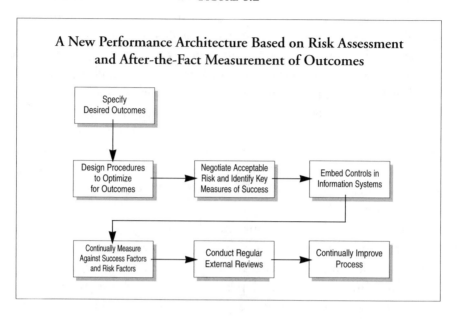

A New Performance Architecture Based on Risk Assessment and After-the-Fact Measurement of Outcomes

Specify Desired Outcomes

Design Procedures to Optimize for Outcomes

Negotiate Acceptable Risk and Identify Key Measures of Success

Embed Controls in Information Systems

Continually Measure Against Success Factors and Risk Factors

Conduct Regular External Reviews

Continually Improve Process

TRUTHS ABOUT MEASURES AND MEASUREMENT: LESSONS LEARNED IN THE TRENCHES

The University of California is perhaps the most complex university on the planet, consisting of eight general research campuses, one health science campus, five medical centers, and management responsibility for three U.S. Department of Energy-funded national laboratories. This university enjoys great renown for academic excellence and is rated by most as the premier graduate research institution in the U.S.

It is no secret that the University of California has struggled in the past decade with seemingly intractable governance and management issues, including frequent and occasionally divisive presidential transitions, a protracted and painful split between the governing board and leadership over affirmative action, frequently turbulent relations with the California legislature, and the general strains associated with providing leadership to diverse and fiercely independent campuses within a historical tradition of deep decentralization and strong shared governance between faculty and administration. In the context of presidential transition, one of a series of task groups assembled under the chairmanship of UCLA Chancellor Charles Young recommended a new program for balancing strong campus desires for increased delegations of business authority, with the growing governmental, regental, and systemwide pressures on accountability. These recommendations, rich in calls for explicit administrative goal setting and outcome measurement, were accepted by incoming UC President J. W. Peltason.

Against this backdrop of administrative and governance uncertainty from 1995 to the present, large numbers of individuals representing nine UC campuses and a host of administrative functions[2] began to implement a new "performance architecture" for UC. This effort was sponsored by Senior Vice President Wayne Kennedy, led by a steering group of campus administrative vice chancellors and system executives, and delivered by task groups representing the major administrative areas of the university. Importantly, this work was cosponsored and supported by IBM Corporation.

Over an 18-month period, over 150 mid- and senior-level university employees engaged in training on measurement and measurement techniques, and developed university-wide vision statements, mission statements, goals, and measures that were aligned among campuses, across functions, and between campuses and the UC system office. Some of the key findings are described as follows.

Measures Demand a Context

While the assertion that measures demand a context may seem axiomatic and hardly qualifies as an insight, this fact is central to the success of any initiative of this kind. It is the author's belief that the central reason for the failure of numerous measurement and assessment initiatives to achieve their planned results stems from either the absence of a context, or the lack of clarity about the measures' intended context.

Measurement contexts vary widely. Measures that are meaningful to operational managers for the purposes of identifying service gaps, or improvement or business opportunities, are likely to have no value to an institution's governing board. Conversely, institution-wide metrics that convey directions and priorities, while contextually necessary to the operating manager, are typically too stratospheric to be actionable without translation into the language of specific institutional subprocesses or functions.

In addition to demanding a level or audience-specific context, measures demand a purpose-specific context. Measures can be used to identify gaps to foster change; they can account for variances between intended outcomes and realized outcomes; they can be used to be used to identify performance trajectories; or measures can diagnose uncontrollable risk factors in the environment, but not all of these measures or uses are interchangeable. The selection of poor measures or the misapplication of useful measurement information by trustees, chancellors, budget officers, and senior executives is responsible for much of the fear and loathing we find associated with this activity. The good news is that as one develops a sensitivity to level specificity in establishing measures, it does become possible to establish measures that are meaningful across diverse institutions. The key lesson learned in this regard is to search for that level of descriptive abstraction that is necessary to render a measure at once meaningful and acceptable to people from diverse institutions. Such an approach is necessary to overcome campuses' intrinsic and largely legitimate tendency to identify their processes, structures, and functions and hence their performance attributes as unique.

For example, one common measure of administrative efficiency in mail management operations is the unit cost of handling per piece of mail. This is a meaningful measure—probably. Armed with data, university leaders are often tempted to compare cost information across institutions and to use such comparisons to create a meaningful managerial context; e.g., "my costs are higher than yours, but lower than theirs." This application of measurement information has a ring of intuitive truth. However, if there exists a campus goal of reducing, through the application of network technologies, the volume of paper-based mail, a campus that is pursuing this goal will likely witness the short-term rise in unit handling costs, as mail volumes decrease at a faster rate than decreases in fixed costs (equipment, space, etc.). In essence, a meaningful measure set in the right context (the campus goal of reducing paper mail volumes) produces a markedly different management outcome (good work!), than the same measure set in the wrong context (e.g., longitudinal: our unit costs are rising; or comparative: their unit costs are lower than ours).

The Most Effective Measurement Context Is that of Institutional Vision and Goals

Many colleges and universities have one-half of a love-hate relationship with strategic planning. Absent a planning context, most campus measurement initiatives run the risk of devolving into time-consuming exercises oriented to answer random and often unimportant questions. The lack of importance of underlying questions, the randomness of the process, the time-consuming nature of the data collection process, and the often punitive application of information obtained leads to resistance at best or, at worst, the fabrication of information. While Deming's notion of driving fear out of management processes may seem trite, it is an essential element of success in implementing effective measurement into planning, assessment, and other management processes.

At the University of California, the stated drive for meaningful measures and the adoption of the Balanced Scorecard™ methodology for developing measures opened a back door to the engagement of the institution in a widespread administrative strategic planning exercise. The Balanced Scorecard™ concept, developed by Kaplan and Norton (1992), is compelling in the manner in which it elucidates two simple ideas: 1) that measures must derive from and support an institutional vision; and 2) that measures must capture the multidimensionality of the enterprise. This latter idea was particularly well-suited to the complexities of the campus environment, particularly in the face of regental or governmental pressures to assess administrative performance on the financial dimension alone (see Figure 6.3).

Figure 6.3

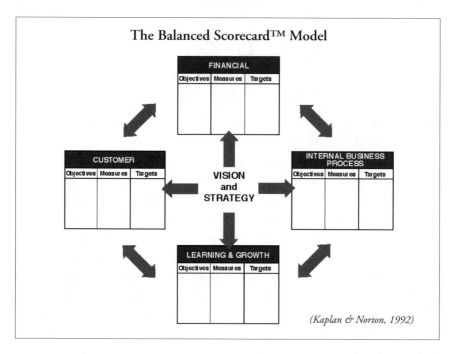

The Balanced Scorecard™ Model

(Kaplan & Norton, 1992)

This approach to organizing measurement information prompted a number of positive actions and outcomes. First, by placing the creation of an enterprise-wide vision and strategies at the center of the task, this approach made it impossible for the university's senior leadership to disengage from or opt out of the project. Once engaged, the dialogue that this process fostered made it necessary and possible to "work" some of the really difficult management and governance of the day; e.g., "How can the university convey its administrative performance story to the Board of Regents?" or "What does it mean to a large, semiautonomous campus like UCLA to be a citizen of a larger University of California?" or "Can [or how can] campus goals and aspirations be accommodated within the context of often very different goals of the system?" These questions go to the very heart of a university's organizational architecture and business model. Second, the Balanced Scorecard™ approach asks very simple and compelling questions that captured the interest of disparate groups of executives and senior operating managers:

- To succeed financially, how must the university appear to our stakeholders?

- To achieve our vision, how should we appear to our customers?

- To satisfy our stakeholders and customers, what business processes must we excel at?

- To achieve our vision, how will we sustain our ability to change and improve?

The vision-centered and multidimensional nature of this approach makes it possible to construct and use measures in ways that communicate the complex tradeoffs intrinsic to colleges and universities in ways that traditional financial metrics alone cannot do. In essence, it provides its users with a quantifiably rich language with which to tell the story of an institutional process or function in ways that can capture and hold the interest of employees (for motivation, direction setting, and personal goal setting); functional and process managers (for direction setting and gap analysis); faculty (who might be customers, resource competitors, or process intermediaries); and executive managers, trustees, and others.[3]

A Hierarchy of Audiences Suggests a Hierarchy of Measures

This is perhaps another axiomatic observation, but one that is too often overlooked. The simple truth is that the nature of information sought by individuals is strongly influenced by their role and by their available time. While the campus purchasing manager should certainly want to know what the cost of a purchasing transaction is for low-value goods acquired, her administrative vice chancellor and chancellor very likely would not. A key insight gleaned from the trenches was one that most of our colleagues in industry, after years of measurement and benchmarking activity, have learned; that is, less is more. This is another reason why numerous industry-wide measurement initiatives in higher education fail. If the marginal cost of creating a measure and collecting and analyzing the associated data is greater than the marginal benefit of the information collected, people will opt out of the process. Industry leaders often refer to the "critical few", those areas of activity for which successful performance ensures the success of the enterprise (at any level) or for which failure puts the enterprise at clear risk. Concentration on the critical few makes broad engagement in measurement activity less onerous and occasionally interesting and most important, focuses attention on those things that are actionable and, in the ideal, that motivate action.

Another key tool adapted for use in the higher education measurement arena to capture this notion of simplification was the executive or board dashboard or cockpit (Figure 6.4). Like the scorecard, dashboards and cockpits are intuitively accessible to busy people and in a short amount of time and space can convey the key stories of an institution's ambitions, struggles, successes, and risks. Unlike the scorecard, which is chiefly a tool for developing and organizing measures and measurement information, the dashboard or cockpit is a tool for communicating not only managerial outcomes, but environmental risks that perhaps cannot be managed (diagnostic measures).

FIGURE 6.4

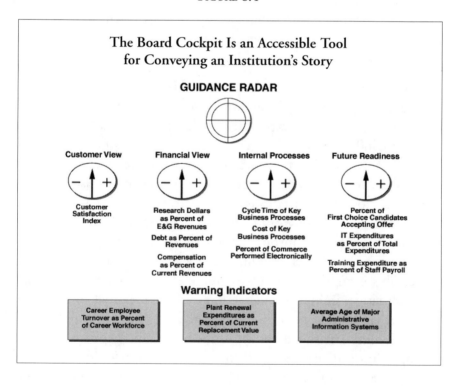

The Board Cockpit Is an Accessible Tool
for Conveying an Institution's Story

GUIDANCE RADAR

Customer View	Financial View	Internal Processes	Future Readiness
Customer Satisfaction Index	Research Dollars as Percent of E&G Revenues	Cycle Time of Key Business Processes	Percent of First Choice Candidates Accepting Offer
	Debt as Percent of Revenues	Cost of Key Business Processes	IT Expenditures as Percent of Total Expenditures
	Compensation as Percent of Current Revenues	Percent of Commerce Performed Electronically	Training Expenditure as Percent of Staff Payroll

Warning Indicators

Career Employee Turnover as Percent of Career Workforce	Plant Renewal Expenditures as Percent of Current Replacement Value	Average Age of Major Administrative Information Systems

Measurement Is a Culturally Dependent Process

And what management process in higher education isn't? While the advisability of measuring transcends industry boundaries and the Balanced Scorecard™ methodology is, at present, chiefly in practice in industry, it is essential to recognize that higher education is unique culturally and that while perhaps our culture is inherently inefficient, it is one that is durable, self-renewing, and rich in the capacity for innovation. For this reason, practitioners of the arcane art of measurement and assessment must account for the unlikelihood that the processes establishing an institutional vision, mission, goals, and associated measures will occur in a classical top-down, cascading fashion. In fact, this process is likely to be highly iterative, resulting in a heightened dialogue and understanding of visions, goals, and measures between and among occupants of different levels of the institutional hierarchy. This process of iteration had a powerful and latent aligning effect on many campus management teams and between campus executives and their counterparts at the system office. A hard lesson to learn in this process was to keep the reins loose. The role of the project leader in this kind of endeavor is to 1) educate, 2) inspire, 3) be relentlessly helpful, and 4) have great faith that engaged and educated people of goodwill will always surpass your expectations.

Outcomes and Conclusions

The experience at the University of California lends credence to the faith shown by those who seek to apply insights about self-organizing biological systems to the realm of management.[4] The results of this activity in some cases corresponded closely to original intentions; e.g., goals and measures were created, collected, analyzed, reported on, and acted on. In other cases, activities stalled along different areas of the journey. In all cases, the latent benefits of the initiative surpassed and, in many cases, exceeded in surprising ways the expectations of the sponsors and leaders of the initiative. Within the project's expected goals, customer satisfaction and organizational climate assessment tools were developed and deployed selectively across the university. With regards to unexpected benefits, one campus has become sufficiently engaged in the methodology that it is exploring the use of the

Balanced Scorecard™ approach to measuring and assessing performance of the academic enterprise proper. In other cases, the very act
of establishing university-wide goals and measures fostered a university-wide commitment to undertake the very painful and difficult
process of assessing the replacement value of each campus's physical
plant, a necessary step to highlighting the university's risk regarding
deferred maintenance. In other cases, newfound intercampus colleagues, in the context of discussing issues related to campus energy
utilization, were motivated to engage, for the first time ever, in collaborative negotiations for energy in the deregulating California energy
market. In all cases, the process of identifying goals, priorities, and
measures of mutual interest fostered deeper understandings and a
heightened interest in common solutions across heterogeneous campus environments. In many cases, the work developed by UC teams
was expanded and elaborated on in national venues, fostering the creation of private consortia for the exchange of campus performance
information for the purpose of benchmarking costs, process attributes, and service levels.

On the governance level, this effort has made some progress in
redefining the relationship of the UC system organization to its campuses and contributed to the passage by the Board of Regents of a
sweeping measure to delegate additional administrative authorities to
the UC campuses.

In sum, measurement is a problematic and increasingly necessary
element of the college and university management tool kit. Measurement has a long and difficult history in the management of higher
education, but can no longer be avoided. The Balanced Scorecard™
concept and methodology have appeal to managers and executives in
higher education and may find application within the academy
proper. Practitioners are encouraged to fight the good fight for the
enhancement and ultimate replacement of transaction control-based
approaches to demonstrating institutional accountability with systems
of diagnostic measures that contain risk, while allowing campus
processes to flow unfettered by in-process check, counterchecks, and

related control techniques that erode process performance. Finally, practitioners are admonished to link measures to institutional vision (or organizational/operational) and goals, to keep measures to a meaningful few that incite positive action, to balance the cost of obtaining information with the value of the information obtained, and to situate measurement information within a story of the institution's issues, aspirations, successes, failures, and risks.

ENDNOTES

1) The current "mania over measures" is not new. See, for example, Seldin, P. (1988). *Evaluating and demonstrating administrative performance.* San Francisco, CA: Jossey-Bass. See also Poulton, N. L. (Ed.). (1981). *Evaluation of management and planning systems: New directions for institutional research, 31.* San Francisco, CA: Jossey-Bass; and Bowen, H. R. (Ed.). (1974). *Evaluating institutions for accountability: New directions for institutional research, 1.* San Francisco, CA: Jossey-Bass. Important contemporary contributors to this dialogue include Massy, W., & Meyerson, J. W. (Eds.). (1994). *Measuring institutional performance in higher education: The Stanford Forum for Higher Education Futures.* Princeton, NJ: Peterson's; and Gaither, G., Nedwek, B. P., & Neal, J. E. (1994). *Measuring up: The promises and pitfalls of performance indicators in higher education, 5.* Washington, DC: ASHE-ERIC Higher Education Reports.

2) Initial activity at UC focused on the areas of payroll, purchasing, disbursements, human resources, facilities management, information resources and computing, environment, and health and safety.

3) In one spectacular instance, one UC campus manager developed campus goals and measures for her department that were linked to university-wide goals, and then linked all individual performance objectives and action plans to these departmental, campus, and enterprise-wide goals and measures.

4) Wheatley, M. J. (1992). *Leadership and the new science: Learning about organization from an orderly universe.* San Francisco, CA: Berrett-Koehler.

REFERENCES

Cohen, M. D., & March, J. G. (1974). *Leadership and ambiguity: The American college president.* New York, NY: McGraw-Hill.

Kaplan, R. S., & Norton, D. P. (1992, January-February). The balanced scoreboard: Measures that drive performance. *Harvard Business Review.*

Keller, G. (1983). *Academic strategy: The management revolution in higher education.* Baltimore, MD: Johns Hopkins University Press.

Massy, W., & Zemsky, R. (1990, June). The lattice and the ratchet. *PEW Policy Perspectives, 2* (4).

Report of the States. (1995, September). Washington, DC: American Association of State Colleges and Universities, p. 1.

Weick, K. E. (1984). Contradictions in a community of scholars: The cohesion-accuracy tradeoff. In J. L. Bess (Ed.), *College and university organization.* New York, NY: New York University Press.

7

Benchmarking in Higher Education

C. Jackson Grayson, Jr.

Most educators agree that the academy faces problems and opportunities of a magnitude that it has never faced before. These challenges are similar to those that business, healthcare, and government all have met in the past few decades. While the restructuring process is underway in these sectors, education lags behind. It's not that those in education don't understand that these problems and opportunities exist, they simply are not adequately responding.

I strongly believe that "benchmarking and implementing best practices" is the most powerful process to assist in restructuring any organization in any sector, but education has not taken advantage of this methodology.

Restructuring cannot be accomplished with a "silver bullet," one methodology that will solve all of its problems overnight. But I have personally seen benchmarking work in business, healthcare, and government, and I am convinced that it can be of valuable assistance to education. I draw this conclusion not from speculation or ideology, but from many years of experience as professor and dean in higher education and several years of involvement with productivity and quality improvement processes at the nonprofit American Productivity & Quality Center (APQC), including actual benchmarking experience through the APQC International Benchmarking Clearinghouse and the APQC Institute for Education Best Practices.

105

I visited 60 education institutes and associations in late 1995 to look for the use of benchmarking in education. My estimate is that 95% of faculty, teachers, and administrators in education are not currently benchmarking, do not know what benchmarking is, or have a misunderstanding about what it is and how it can improve their overall performance.

Understanding Benchmarking

Definition of Benchmarking

Benchmarking is the process of identifying, learning, adapting, and implementing outstanding practices and processes from organizations anywhere in the world to help an organization improve its performance. More simply stated: Benchmarking is "finding and adapting best practices."

Misunderstandings and Clarifications about Benchmarking

As important as it is to understand what benchmarking is, it is equally important to understand what benchmarking is not. There are several common misunderstandings and misuse of the terms "benchmarks," "benchmarking," and "best practices."

Both "benchmarks" and "benchmarking" are important, but they are not the same. Benchmarks are outcomes such as numbers, measures, and standards, identifying the gap between where you are and where others are, while benchmarking is the process, or best practices, used to achieve those benchmarks.

The following clarifies some common misunderstandings about benchmarking.

- *It is not copying.* Rarely can anyone take a best practice and directly copy it into their own organization. It must be adapted.

- *It is not spying or espionage.* Benchmarking is done openly and with cooperation and collaboration with the organization being studied.

- *It is not scapegoating and blaming.* It is about finding information for improvement.

■ *It is not just reading articles, case studies, or abstracts of best practices.* These help, but written materials never really describe how processes work in actual practice. Learning the tacit knowledge, culture, structure, and enablers takes personal involvement, conversation, observation, and interaction. Benchmarking is action learning.

■ *It is not just networking through conferences, coffee breaks, telephone conversations, or browsing the Internet.* Networking is useful and often a prelude to benchmarking, but it is no substitute for action learning, involvement, participation, direct observation, and site visits.

■ *It is not quick or easy.* Identifying, learning, adapting, and implementing best practices is neither quick nor easy. It is hard work and takes time.

■ *There is not one unique "best" practice.* A frequently asked question is "How do you know who or what is best?" Rarely is one single best found in business, healthcare, government, or education. "Best" is a relative word and what is best in one setting is not necessarily best in another.

"Best practices" are those practices (there may be four, five, or more) judged to be "exemplary," "better," "good," or "successfully demonstrated." Most benchmarkers first work out a set of criteria for what they would judge to be "best" or "excellent." To help them arrive at a selected set of practices, they then look to literature research, surveys, peer and customer evaluations, site visits, and as much quantitative and qualitative data as they can.

HOW TO BENCHMARK

Benchmarking is a systematic and disciplined process that requires specific steps to yield maximum knowledge and implementation. AT&T has 12 steps in its benchmarking process, Xerox has 10, Weyerhaueser has 33, and the American Productivity & Quality Center (APQC) has four.

Regardless of the number of steps, each requires the following essential elements:

1) Selecting key processes critical to achieving the vision, mission, standards, and goals of your organization

2) Analyzing how you are now doing those processes

3) Identifying others who are doing the process better or best

4) Learning how they are performing their process

5) Adapting and implementing the process to your own organization

6) Selecting another process and repeating

Mistakes that are easy to make that will diminish the results:

- Selecting processes that are interesting, popular, easy to do, but that are not critical to achieving your vision

- Failing to understand and document how you are doing it now

- Not searching broadly for who is doing it better or best; the search should span your own institution, other education institutions, business, healthcare, or government in the U.S. and internationally

- Only obtaining explicit (cognitive) data and information, overlooking very important tacit (noncognitive) knowledge and enablers that are essential for implementation

- Failing to involve your own process owners from the beginning and failing to adapt the best practice process to your own organization

- Failing to implement

Of these, perhaps the most common mistake educators make is to only benchmark with other educational institutions, and usually only with institutions like themselves—research institutions with research institutions, liberal arts with liberal arts institutions, etc. In doing so they miss out on some of the most important potential breakthrough best practices from other sectors.

Initially, business, government, and healthcare commonly also believed that they could only learn the best practices from their own industry, and from organizations of the same size, culture, location, etc. However, it is now commonplace for any organization in business, healthcare, or government to learn from any other organization. They have found some of the best practices by looking outside the box to other sectors.

St. Luke's Hospital has learned from the Ritz-Carlton. Xerox has learned from L.L. Bean. The Air Force has learned from AT&T. Citibank has learned from Hewlett-Packard. Cornell University learned from Westark Community College and the New Brunswick Telephone Company. Such cross-sector benchmarking typically leads to new ways to do things, to higher goals, and to an acceleration of change.

BENEFITS TO EDUCATION FROM BENCHMARKING

If education follows these steps, while avoiding major mistakes, the evidence is clear from thousands of benchmarking projects in other sectors that major benefits can be achieved.

- Improvement in quality, productivity, outcomes, customer satisfaction, and reduced costs.

- Acceleration of restructuring and change.

- Prevention of costly "reinvention" when someone else has found a better way. Many improvements are approached as though they had never been done before by anyone anywhere. Failure to use already known best practices could doom education.

- Discovery of breakthroughs and new paradigms that yield not just incremental small changes, but quantum changes.

- Creation of a sense of urgency when the size of performance gaps are shown to exist. "I don't think we knew how bad we were until we benchmarked," said the owner of one business. It knocks you off your complacency stool.

- Help in overcoming inertia, skepticism, complacency, and resistance to change. Benchmarking serves as an organizational change process. As Hal Tragash of Xerox said about benchmarking, "The only way we convinced most managers of a new way was to allow them to witness it with their own eyes. Talking to them about it didn't do the trick."

■ Speeding up of dissemination of innovation and best practices, benchmarking deploys good ideas faster and moves them to scale quicker.

■ Evidence for setting higher, but attainable, goals for improvement based on objective evidence that such outcomes have been achieved elsewhere.

■ Forced examinations of an organization's own processes, which in itself can lead to improvements, and help in prioritizing improvement activities.

■ Greater likelihood of implementation of best practices because of direct participation by process owners.

■ Objective information valuable for strategic planning, resource allocation, or reallocation.

■ Support for culture changes to become an outward looking organization, opposed to one that is internally focused.

■ Creation of sharing networks for future benchmarking and continuous learning and improvement.

These benefits can be achieved by the smallest and the largest education institutions: Ivy League schools, community colleges, complex research institutions, technology institutions, liberal arts, and elementary and secondary schools. Everyone can improve regardless of their location, mission, wealth, or national standing.

How does benchmarking achieve these benefits when other methods fall short or die from faddism?

■ From participation by those who must make the change. The owners of the process, whether they are faculty, students, administrators, or parents—not staff or a group of outside experts—are involved.

- Through active, not passive learning. Learning as a participant, not as a spectator. Learning in context, not abstracted into generality. Learning for use and action. As Alfred North Whitehead said, "Knowledge without action is useless."

- Through decision-making that is driven by data. Ideology, hearsay, and personal bias are not used to make decisions.

- By going outside one's own sector. Fresh, breakthrough ideas are obtained.

- Through acceleration of change. Change occurs more rapidly and easily because of the direct involvement, and also because it helps to convince skeptics who see that others are not only doing it differently, but getting better results. As Bob George, benchmarking manager at duPont, noted, "Benchmarking is a change management process, and the one we use at duPont."

- Through being a continuous process, rather than a one-shot technique.

One reaction I've gotten from educators is that while benchmarking might work in business, healthcare, and government, education is different. It doesn't fit. I differ.

The benchmarking process relates directly to the core values of education—learning, scientific inquiry, data-based decision-making, participation, open communication, learning by discovery, teaming, and collegial sharing. For example, consider the steps followed in benchmarking and those in learning.

Learning	Benchmarking
What do I want to learn?	What do I want to benchmark?
Why learn it?	Why benchmark it?
What do I know?	What do I know?
How can I learn it?	How can I benchmark it?
Who can I learn it from?	Who can I benchmark with?
What did I learn?	What did I learn?
How can I apply it?	How can I apply it?

Why Education Lags Behind in Benchmarking

If benchmarking is so great, why hasn't education embraced benchmarking?

1) Many in education are still in denial, arguing that there really isn't a problem and no reason exists to change. Years ago, many organizations in business, healthcare, and government did the same; firms like GM, Sears, IBM, and RCA either failed or almost went over the edge. Those that survived finally admitted the problems and restructured.

Most educators (with exceptions) haven't yet recognized and are not responding to the growing frustration, restlessness, and anger of their stakeholders. Nor do they acknowledge the power of competitive threats like distance education, for-profit universities, and corporate universities. Most live in the old paradigm, so their response, if any, has been to cut budgets, launch cost-cutting drives, drop programs, or defer expenses. They haven't yet had to change and are blinded—as were the other sectors—by a false sense of security.

2) Many reject benchmarking, labeling it as a business tool that has no applicability in education, because "a university is not a business." That is true. But the similarities are as great as the differences, and both can learn from one another. Still, many academics fear benchmarking as a Trojan horse designed by business to worm their way into the university, run it like a business, and interfere with academic freedom.

3) Most equate benchmarking with only benchmarks (numbers) and stop there. They omit the necessary benchmarking steps that are essential for implementation and change.

4) Many say they are benchmarking when they go to conferences, attend seminars, read case studies or a book on best practices, or talk to one another at meetings or on the phone. In a way, they are benchmarking. But these relatively informal steps typically fail to involve other process owners and don't gather data and knowledge essential for acceptance and implementation.

5) Change is difficult in every sector, but especially hard in centuries-old education. Most of the educational traditions, habits, tenure, and sense of history reinforce status quo and continuity, not continuous improvement.

6) Educators have a preference of learning only from other educational institutions and especially those similar to them. They do not look at dissimilar education institutions (e.g., community colleges) where a great amount of innovation and restructuring is taking place. Many educators from prestige liberal arts universities, for example, have told me they could learn nothing from community colleges or technological institutions. For this same reason, most educators do not even think of looking outside of education for best practices.

7) Educators have a preference for discussion and debate of issues, rather than change and action. There is a focus on activity, not results. Few changes occur only from dialogue, committees, task forces, exhortation, retreats, or just information. Benchmarking focuses on implementation from the start.

8) Educators fear that they will be punished if benchmarking results show others to have better practices and outcomes, as opposed to believing that it will be used for improvement. So they do not benchmark, or they suppress the results if it makes them look bad.

9) Most educators have had no knowledge of how to do disciplined, systematic benchmarking, nor do they want to take the time to learn, stating that they are already too busy and overworked. Convinced that they are doing the best they can, that no one could be working harder, they fall prey to the deception that there is not much useful to learn from anyone else and they don't have time to explore. The other sectors said similar things in the beginning, but later realized that best practices could save them time and release them for what they really want to do.

10) Educators and educational reformers seem to believe that benchmarking is not needed to spread best practices, that best practices will somehow spontaneously diffuse. They will automatically spread. As the Consortium on Productivity in the Schools pointed out in a 1995 report, "Unfortunately, several empirical studies,

beginning as far back as 1972, have discredited that theory." Demonstrated better practices do not automatically diffuse among universities or K-12 schools. Many isolated innovations and promising reforms typically remain just that—laudable and promising islands of best practices that fail to alter old paradigms.

11) At the heart of benchmarking (and quality) is the concept of focusing on the customer, and benchmarking those customer-driven processes. But the concept of "customers" and the use of feedback from customers to improve is foreign to most educators who have a producer, not a customer focus. As Drucker—himself an academician—points out, "The purpose of an organization resides outside itself." Benchmarking requires an organization to look outside itself.

12) Educators have a preference for focusing on process (inputs and activities) only, believing that if the process is right, the right outcomes will follow. Benchmarking requires that both processes and outcomes be examined. The fallacy in the process-only view is that while the process may be just right, the outcomes may not be what the market wants. Buggy whip manufacturers did not survive by improving processes. Pony Express riders did not survive by getting faster horses. Nevertheless, many educators remain focused on improving processes and do not benchmark outcomes.

13) Educators have a strong attachment to explicit (codifiable) cognitive information about best practices that comes from books, articles, and pamphlets. While these are valuable and need to be encouraged, they omit tacit (noncodifiable) information that can only be gained by observation and conversation. Many educators are uncomfortable and unprepared to do this kind of benchmarking because they never learned that way themselves. They don't know "how to learn" any other way. They focus on codified and omit key how-to tacit knowledge.

14) Those education institutions that already think they are the best see no reason to benchmark. Alas, history is replete with the downfall of nations whose success generated complacency, and who fell because of the "victory" or "affluence" disease. Many of America's top firms learned that lesson the hard way and failed. But successful leaders no longer make that mistake. Jack Welch, chairman of General

Electric, the world's largest U.S. corporation in market value, says, "No more of this not-invented-here stuff. We'll take ideas from anywhere, deploy them, and use them as quickly as we can." Sad to say— the same is not true today of most of the leading education institutions. As Somerset Maugham put it, "Only mediocre people are always at their best."

15) Effective process benchmarking occurs with cross-functional teams of people in order to get "buy-in" and implementation. Yet, most educators work in isolation from one another and with a wide gulf between academic disciplines and administrative and academic processes. These rigid silos block effective benchmarking.

16) Most educators mistakenly believe that benchmarking will only work for administrative processes and not the teaching/learning process. Thus, benchmarking is consigned to the "business" side of the university, thereby blocking major gains achievable for the heart of the university/enterprise.

17) Some educators assert that benchmarking won't work because every institution is different; that they have to deal with a multitude of stakeholders; and work with students vastly different in skills, intelligence, motivation, age, etc. Physicians said the same in the beginning: "Benchmarking won't work, for everything is unique. We have to deal with patients of vastly different physical, social, races, ages, prior medical histories, emotional strengths, etc." Leading healthcare practitioners and institutions are now benchmarking with one another and other sectors, focusing on processes, and adjusting for preexisting conditions so that risk-adjusted outcomes can be calculated. Educators could do the same by focusing on processes and by assessing prior learning and ending outcomes.

SUGGESTIONS FOR GETTING STARTED

Every one of these reasons why education is doing extremely little benchmarking can be overcome. Organizations in other sectors either have changed or are changing, and benchmarking has been useful in doing so. David Kearns, former chairman of Xerox, attributed Xerox's improved competitiveness to two underpinnings: "... employee involvement and benchmarking."

If you decide—and I hope you do—to become involved in benchmarking, here are a few steps to get started.

1) Take at least two days of benchmarking training. Later on, take more.

2) Discuss and explain the use of benchmarking, as distinguished from "benchmarks," to those involved in the process.

3) Discuss in your organization what are the critical processes in which you want improvement—both administrative and academic processes. Don't benchmark everything. Tie the benchmarking to achieving the vision of the institution, not a tool to be applied whether it fits or not.

4) Follow the key steps for benchmarking, either individually in your own organization or with a benchmarking consortium.

INSTITUTE FOR EDUCATION BEST PRACTICES

In 1996, APQC created the Institute for Education Best Practices, an offshoot of APQC's International Benchmarking Clearinghouse (IBC) that had formed in 1992, to help education organizations benchmark best practices.

- IBC was designed by 86 corporations who saw the need for benchmarking assistance through a clearinghouse.

- IBC has 500 members, including 60% of the Fortune 100 firms, 35 federal government agencies, and 400 other business, government, and healthcare firms. Only three members are from higher education and one from a school district.

- IBC has members in the U.S., Canada, Mexico, Asia, Europe, and South America.

- IBC has conducted 250 benchmarking projects and trained 10,000 people in benchmarking in over 30 nations.

Using the IBC's experience and knowledge as a base, APQC created the Institute for Education Best Practices to encourage and assist education institutions in benchmarking—not just with other education institutions, but also with business, healthcare, and government.

The institute uses a consortium study model, in which 10 to 20 organizations agree to be sponsors of a benchmarking study of a particular process and become personally involved in the process.

- Each sponsor commits at least two persons to the study, who hold a day-and-a-half meeting to scope the study, decide on the criteria for selection of best practices, and nominate possible best practice organizations.

- The institute screens potential best practice organizations by conducting primary and secondary research to collect data on potential best practice organizations. The information is blinded and sent to participants.

- The participants select five to six organizations to visit, and then design a questionnaire for the site visits. Institute staff and the participants then conduct the site visits.

- Participants come together for a last meeting of both the sponsors and the best practice organizations for a final sharing session. Each sponsor is invited to bring up to five persons with them to hear the final presentation and network. The site visit reports and a list of key findings are presented.

This same process has been used for over 50 consortium studies by IBC with business, healthcare, and government and is now being used with education organizations.

By mid-1997 the institute completed two major benchmarking studies in higher education and began another which was completed in October 1997. Over 50 sponsoring higher education organizations, none of which had done systematic benchmarking before, participated in the studies. One study focused on budgeting, another on electronic student services, and the third on measuring institutional performance outcomes.

1) Institutional budgeting. Ten colleges and universities studied best practices in budgeting for six months, using IBC's methodology. Bill Massy of Stanford University was the "subject matter expert." Participating in the study were research universities, community colleges, liberal arts, and technology-oriented institutions. Each organization

committed two people to the study, and they benchmarked best practices in budgeting, selecting four education institutions, a hospital, and a pharmaceutical company as places to visit.

2) Creating electronic student services. This benchmarking study was done in partnership with SHEEO (State Higher Education Executive Officers). Sixteen colleges and universities participated, together with two software firms and one consulting firm. The subject matter expert was Mary Beth Sussman, president of the Colorado Electronic Community College. The group visited four educational institutions, a hotel chain, and a telephone company in New Brunswick, Canada.

3) Measuring institutional performance outcomes. Twenty colleges and universities participated in an October 1997 study, with Peter Ewell of NCHEMS as the subject matter expert.

With very few exceptions, evaluations by participants in these studies have been almost unanimously positive.

Many others studies began in late 1997: Measuring Learning Outcomes, Corporate Universities, and Resource Reallocation. Others likely to begin in 1998 are Technology in Teaching/Learning, Faculty Roles and Rewards, Distance Learning, Post-Tenure Review, Capital Projects Planning, Learning Productivity, Change Management, Strategic Planning, and Student Advising.

In addition to conducting more consortium studies, the institute launched two other major activities in late 1997.

Knowledge Base of Education Best Practices. These abstracts of best practices are not only from institute benchmarking studies, but from other sources. This knowledge base will also be linked to other best practice databases in education, business, government and healthcare—not only in the U.S., but internationally. It will use an education process classification framework created jointly with Arthur Andersen to serve as a taxonomy for the classification of best practices. This knowledge base is expected to be globally accessible through the Internet.

Facilitator Network. This national network includes part-time (10% to 20% of their time) facilitators who are knowledge brokers in their own institutions. Their functions are twofold: 1) observe, collect, and codify best practices in their own organizations and forward these to the knowledge base, and 2) assist faculty and administrators in their own organization to improve by identifying and using best practices. These facilitators will be trained, linked electronically with one another, and occasionally will meet face to face. The idea for this network of facilitators was adapted from a similar network used by Texas Instruments to collect, disseminate, and help implement best practices inside TI.

CONCLUSION

I am both a lover and a critic of higher education. As John Gardner pointed out, there are "unloving critics" who bash, slash, and see no good in institutions. There are also "uncritical lovers" who overlook faults and magnify successes. I classify myself as a "critical lover" who respects and loves education, but who must also be honestly critical to help it improve and survive.

It is in my role as a critical lover that I highly recommend that all education institutions overcome their isolation and inertia, and engage in benchmarking—and implementing—best practices from education, business, healthcare, and government. However, benchmarking won't solve every problem; neither is it an end in itself. But it is a powerful vehicle for improvement to achieve education's objectives and values. It is deceptively simple in concept, complex in reality, and rich in results.

REFERENCES

Consortium on Productivity in the Schools. (1995, October). *Using what we have to get the schools we need: A productivity focus for American education.* New York, NY: The Institute on Education and the Economy, Teachers College, Columbia University.

8

Higher Education's Information Challenge

Marshall W. Van Alstyne

INTRODUCTION

Universities process information. They create, teach, cache, and accredit it. In an information economy, their roles in refining information might move us to value them as essential resources. Ironically, however, the level of public funding would not necessarily mark higher education as an investment priority even though the information economy continues to expand. The Internet experiences triple digit growth annually, virtual communities form around "collaboratories," web browsers now deliver customized news from *The New York Times,* and software companies enjoy price to earnings ratios that are four times those of auto manufacturers. Yet, between 1980-1995, federal funds to postsecondary schools declined by 14% (Hoffman, 1995). Why should universities, as processors of information, not share in the associated profits and prestige of the information age?

"Creative destruction" might account for some of this inconsistency. The price of information technology (IT) has declined by an order of magnitude relative to its price per cycle 15 years ago (Brynjolfsson, 1993). IT enables long distance learning, nonjudgmental and infinitely patient mentoring, and public access to vast information resources. In the argot of the economists, perhaps technology is a substitute for the university good. Between substitutes, declining prices for one then force proportional cuts in the other. This might even explain growing consumption of educational goods and services as prices of nontraditional substitutes become increasingly affordable. Or perhaps, based on laws of supply and demand, "a world awash in information is one in which information has very little market value" (Krugman, 1996). Universities, as information delivery systems, face a growing challenge to convey information products that can be obtained elsewhere at negligible cost to the source. Information is unique in that its giver still keeps the gift.

These dour observations, however, only partially describe the forces acting on universities and they often underestimate university contributions to social welfare. Access to information, for example, only weakly substitutes for access to education and expertise. When faced with a complex and time sensitive legal problem, technological access to a good law library is no substitute for a well-educated lawyer. Complex environments typically increase the demand for skilled labor. On the welfare side, various studies of the economics of science have found that knowledge stocks—as measured by publication counts and scientific employment—contributed substantially to productivity in 18 industries and that each of several major innovations—magnetic ferrites, videotape recorders, oral contraceptives, electron microscopes, and matrix isolation—depended on research that emphasized basic understanding over applications (Stephan, 1996). What remains underappreciated is that these studies found that lags of 20 to 30 years obscured the connection between knowledge and productivity.

One notable scholar has written of the "dim future of the university" (Noam, 1995), while Drucker has argued that traditional colleges will become relics in the 21st century (Lenzer & Johnson, 1997). Changing technology and environments imply that universities need to adapt since traditional structures face too many nontraditional needs. There is reason for optimism, however. Few scholars, if any, have argued that universities provide no value or that collectively we have no influence. If anything, the moral of new technology is that it gives us new options and we must choose how to use it.

This essay seeks to identify technology and information forces acting on universities, to offer an economic justification for continued public support, and to suggest an organizational modification that might enhance their success. Doing this involves sketching the university as an information processor in order to guide questions, highlight options, and formulate possible answers. If our primary goal is to build a better university—and universities process information—then it helps to know which factors improve information processing.

ASSUMPTIONS

My working assumptions about universities focus on the information per se in order to model a particular view of their operations. There are other models of how universities operate but I want to abstract away from the particulars of individual institutions and examine the economy of ideas and their delivery in the context of teaching and research.

Information Processes Are Integral to University Functions

Universities create, warehouse, distribute, and evaluate information. As houses of research, they generate new information. Their libraries store not only the results of their working papers and interim reports but also the publications essential for teaching and learning. In the process of teaching, they disseminate new and existing information. Through education, they inculcate students with methods, tests, facts, and representations. Then, as arbiters of information quality, university faculty referee new publications. By conferring degrees, universities attest to the quality of the information that new graduates seek to apply professionally. Broadly speaking, this is an assumption that viewing universities as information processors helps understand what universities do.

Technology Improvements Simplify Information Processing

Information technology (IT) facilitates searching, screening, storing, and connecting. IT aids computation. Whether this is good or bad for universities depends, in part, on whether IT substitutes for university functions or complements them. Declining costs of a substitute can reduce demand for the university good while declining costs of a complement can increase it. To the extent that both phenomena are present, one success strategy might be to emphasize university functions that are complements of IT and to avoid functions that are substitutes.

Information Is "Nonrival"

This is the most crucial assumption. When two or more consumers simultaneously attempt to use rival assets, they can physically displace one another. Unlike tangible goods, nonrival assets are neither depleted nor divided when shared, and they can be reproduced almost limitlessly. Because of information's nonrival quality, people can give it away without actually losing it themselves. A professor, for example, does not lose her knowledge by telling students what she knows; her understanding may even improve. And, by inference, information once given can never be withdrawn.

Of course, the nonrival question of depleting information differs from the economic question of valuing information. Value may still depend on scarcity or even ubiquity. Stock price leads, for example, decrease in value as they are distributed but computer operating systems increase. Nonrivalry only refers to the property of negligible cost copying. This assumption is also distinct from "excludability," which represents a de jure proscription rather than a de facto ability to prevent others from using an asset (e.g., trade laws protect accessible but patented information).

People Are Boundedly Rational

As finite creatures, we have a limited capacity for mental calculation (Simon, 1957). We can optimize only a few polynomial equations in our heads; can listen to no more than a few people at one time; and can read only a finite number of books in a lifetime. Information technology can loosen the bounds on rationality but will not lift them entirely. The Internet can provide access to millions of other users and a wide range of knowledge sources, but no one person can interact with them all.

Consider that as of May 1996, the AltaVista search engine had indexed more that 33 million articles and web pages. It would take over five years to read just the new listings added each month. Even if information technology were to double our individual capacities, we would need to draw the line on our threshold of interest somewhere. The information we seek, read, review, and comprehend is finite. Computationally, the number of our simultaneous conversations is also finite. Information technology is unlikely to permit individuals to widen their focus to the entire population. As M. Dertouzos says, "You can [have access] to hundreds of millions, but you can't know them all because all you can remember is 3000. All you can do is replace the label 'physical acquaintance' with 'virtual acquaintance'" (Rowe, 1996). Bounded rationality simply means that we will need to make choices about which information to process, and live with the long-term results of these choices. For purposes of this essay, I will take bounded rationality to mean that there are limits on computation and that there are a finite number of partners that anyone can speak with at any given time.

CONVEX GROWTH AND THE INFORMATION EXPLOSION

These assumptions are all that is necessary—or very nearly so—to account for an information explosion. The point is to understand why this is happening and then to anticipate and manage the consequences. Vastly increasing the amount of new information has significant implications for a university's structure, specialization, reward systems, and reputation. Nonrivalry can help to explain an information explosion.

The basic argument is analogous to that for compound interest and relies on recovering the inputs to production after production is finished. If more input can be used to produce more output, but the input is never actually consumed, then each new period faces an increased level of resources with which to produce (Romer, 1986, 1990). The new growth literature in economics depends on this mechanism. Knowledge generated through research at one firm spills over to increased productivity at other firms, and all firms benefit

from a rise in the total knowledge stock. Under certain reasonable economic assumptions, the knowledge stock then grows at an increasing rate.

The truth is much more complicated than this. In reality, no exponential nor even convex process can continue unabated. Moreover, any form of production must involve labor and capital of some sort and these more tangible resources are clearly bounded, maybe even consumed, in the process. Therefore, any serious model of information will be bounded by tangible resources or by constraints such as bounded rationality. As a stylized abstraction, however, this simple model reflects apparent growth in information resources surprisingly well. Two examples illustrate. Beginning in 1907, the Chemical Abstracts Society took 31 years to accumulate its first million abstracts, the next million took 18 years, and the most recent took 1.75. More articles have been published on chemistry in the last two years than all of recorded history before 1900 (Noam, 1995). Broadening our focus from chemical abstracts to published research, the same phenomenon holds (see Figure 8.1). Near linear growth on this log scale shows that volumes at private research libraries have grown exponentially during most of the 20th century.

FIGURE 8.1

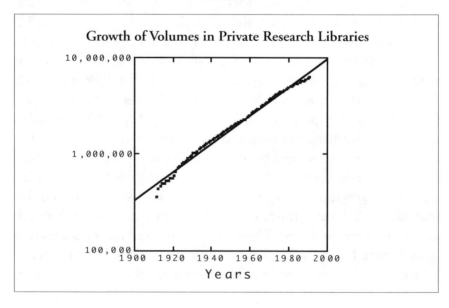

Since the graph has logarithmic scale, the upward sloping line indicates increasing rates of growth over a period of more than 80 years (Cummings et al., 1992). De Sola Pool found similar exponential growth in information generated by the mass media (Pool, 1983).

Setting aside the modeling details, what could be the engine of information growth? Business and economic literature suggest that explicit sharing behaviors play the lead role. Speaking of "intelligent enterprises," one management scholar writes:

> ... knowledge is one of the few assets that grows most [when] shared. As one shares knowledge with colleagues, ... not only do [they] gain information ... they usually feed back questions, amplifications, and modifications, which ... add further value for the [sharer] .... Since learning feeds knowledge back to the base, the next step (even at the same percentage increase) will spring from a higher base and be a larger absolute increment (Quinn, 1992).

In the economics literature, Romer (1986) argues that knowledge spillovers and unintentional sharing enhance the knowledge stock. Imperfect patents and labor transfers can mean that one company's research also leads to other companies' products. A case study by Annalee Saxenian (1994) provides the general theory with empirical support. Beginning in 1975, California's Silicon Valley and Massachusetts' Route 128 region employed roughly the same number of people, but over the next 15 years Silicon Valley generated three times as many net new technology jobs. Moreover, between 1986 and 1990, the market value of the Silicon Valley firms increased by more than $25 billion as compared to $1 billion along Route 128. Saxenian argues that information sharing and collaboration account for most of this difference, with several factors emerging as explanatory variables. First, a higher level of vertical integration in New England firms reduced information transfers between markets and business units. Second, more defense funding led to a premium on secret research which could not be shared. Third, engineering and technical expertise moved more freely in California's open and spirited environment. Adjacent to Silicon Valley, Stanford University also stimulated infor-

mation transfers by hosting on-site executive education programs, charging companies $10,000 for university access, and opening a technology licensing office in 1969. In contrast, Saxenian argues, MIT inadvertently limited information transfers by requiring students to be on campus, charging $50,000 for university access, and neglecting their licensing office until the late 1980s. These forces greatly increased the volume of information sharing in Silicon Valley, subsequently compounding regional wealth.

Interestingly, this model of knowledge compounding might also help to explain the increasing inequality among cohorts of research scientists.

> ... scientific productivity is not only characterized by extreme inequality at a point in time, it is also characterized by increasing inequality over the careers of a cohort of scientists, suggesting that at least some of the processes at work are state dependent (Stephan, 1996).

If the generation of new knowledge requires research resources, and access to knowledge is critical among them, then above average access might lead to above average (and growing) productivity. Universities play a significant role in providing the intellectual and physical capital that make scientific research possible.

From these observations, three significant points can be taken away regarding information processes and the university. Growth in information resources has proceeded at a prodigious rate; theories of information suggest that its nonrival property facilitates growth through sharing; and university processes can affect both the distribution and sharing of information that drive these outcomes.

SPECIALIZATION AND FRAGMENTATION

As a consequence of rapidly expanding information, boundedly rational processors eventually hit the limits of their capacity. As Herb Simon suggests, "a wealth of information creates a poverty of attention and a need to allocate that attention efficiently among the overabundance of information sources that might consume it" (Simon, 1973). From the perspective of research and teaching, advancing the

frontiers of a discipline becomes easier as you narrow your focus sufficiently to master the facts, methods, and principles of the scholarship
that has preceded you. As one's own discipline becomes richer, more
detailed, and more complex, Renaissance scholarship in the sense of
being an authority on the latest developments in unrelated disciplines
becomes more difficult. Producing frontier research in the context of
rapidly expanding information thus encourages specialization.

Numerous academic disciplines exhibit increasingly narrow focus.
In fact, many have progressed to the point where the specialized
vocabulary that facilitates interactions within the community hinders
interaction across communities. Indeed, Kuhn has observed that a
widening gulf "separates the professional scientist from his colleagues
in other fields" (Kuhn, 1970). Mathematicians unfamiliar with the
theory of "elliptic curves" from the subfield of algebraic geometry, for
example, cannot follow a recent proof of Fermat's last theorem. Splin-
ter groups at academic conferences now testify to their increasing differentiation from the core. Differentiation and inbreeding has progressed to the point where expertise can mean "knowing more and
more about less and less."

By increasing communications reach, information technology can
compound specialization. Scholars have an incentive to keep abreast
of new developments by keeping in touch with other scholars
researching related topics. If IT provides a lubricant that allows for the
satisfaction of preferences against the friction of geography, then more
IT can imply that scholars increasingly fulfill their preferences. A preference for research contact that is more focused than contacts available locally leads to narrower interactions. Importantly, the opposite is
also true. A preference for diverse contacts leads to broader interactions and more integrated communities. Technology creates options
but preferences create outcomes. Preferences, in this case, significantly
affect community integration with narrow preferences leading to fragmentation and broad preferences leading to integration.

Because the Internet makes it easier to find colleagues with common research interests, it can facilitate and strengthen focused communities that are dispersed geographically. Thus, sociologists, particle
physicists, political scientists, and others have used the Internet to

find each other and swap information. Communities can also coalesce around resources. Long distance access, for example, allows inland oceanographers to read from the equipment and data sets of their coastal colleagues.

If a mathematician increasingly works with colleagues across the continent, what happens to his or her interactions with the physicist, the biologist, and the historian who work down the hall? Figure 8.2 shows graphically how several local communities could be reshaped by information technology.

FIGURE 8.2

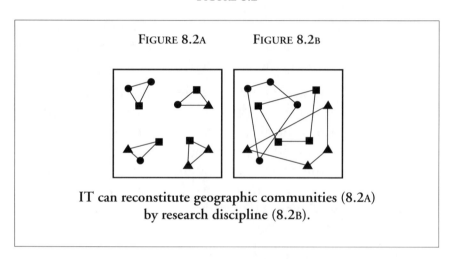

FIGURE 8.2A   FIGURE 8.2B

IT can reconstitute geographic communities (8.2A)
by research discipline (8.2B).

On-campus heterogeneity can give way to off-campus homogeneity as virtual communities coalesce across geographic boundaries. This can simultaneously strengthen alliances to a professional community as it weakens alliances to the university's infrastructure. Research communities can become disembodied with respect to institutional locales. As IT improves filtering, tailoring, segmenting, and searching, the more global network can become the less local village.

There are definite exceptions. Specialization is partly a response to the problem of processing one information type more efficiently—high volume processing implied by efficient specialization. This also depends, however, on relatively low variance in processing types. Flux in the environment may favor more flexible or general skills (Van

Alstyne, 1998) and broader interaction. Increased reach, as provided by IT, can also reverse tendencies toward community fragmentation. Any taste for diverse interactions can lead scholars into contact with new communities which could integrate rather than divide their respective disciplines. Incentives thus provide key leverage. Frequently, for example, promotion and tenure incentives favor specialization and narrow focus. Integration versus fragmentation then hinges on factors such as whether the pressure to publish at the frontier of one's own discipline is low enough to permit time for exploration in others. If keeping abreast of new developments occupies more of one's time, then less time remains for exploration, leaving the net effect as increased fragmentation. IT's capacity to strengthen in-group and weaken out-group ties has been observed by communications researchers such as Edward Mabry:

> Historically, the strength of an academic department rested with its resident faculty. Now it depends on the extent to which each faculty member is interconnected with other professionals—worldwide—pursuing similar interests.... We now have electronic research teams and electronic water coolers. This drastically changes—weakens, in my opinion—indigenous workplace relationships and affects workplace cohesiveness (Leslie, 1995).

Related observations appear to hold more broadly. In describing what characterizes the emerging "global village," McLuhan and Powers (1989) nevertheless remark on the power of satellite technology to aid "super-regionalisms" and "separatisms" like the Parti Quebeçois in Canada. As an historical example, the telephone strengthened affiliation among teenage peer groups (Sproull & Kiesler, 1991). In the field of economics, the number of out-of-state and out-of-country coauthorships in four top journals grew from 4.6% in the 1960s to 27.6% in the 1990s (Gaspar & Glaeser, 1996).

Overspecialization could have the effect of erecting virtual walls between scholarly communities, diminishing worthwhile interaction that currently takes place. Watson and Crick, for example, combined skills from zoology and x-ray diffraction to determine the structure of DNA (Moffat, 1993). Thomas Kuhn developed his ideas on scientific paradigm shifts while working at the nexus of history and physics; yet one can hardly imagine the difficulty of trying to look across paradigms from within. Once Black and Scholes recognized their formula for options pricing as a physics equation for heat transfer (Black & Scholes, 1973), they could look for established parallels. Wall Street now hires dozens of physicists annually and, conceivably, reducing knowledge spillovers could have stalled the development of options markets. Similarly, the Alvarez theory that an asteroid caused the extinction of the dinosaurs emerged from a fortuitous combination of father and son skills in astrophysics and geology. Their inquiry began with the realization that iridium—an element rare on earth but common in asteroids—appears in the geological record in concentrations 20 to 160 times background levels at the time the dinosaurs became extinct (Alvarez, 1980). In significant breakthroughs, serendipity may also play a role since it is often unclear beforehand which groups need to share information. Both the heat transfer equation and knowledge of mass extinctions had existed for more than a century. The Alvarez contribution was not to discover a phenomenon but to combine phenomena, providing the best explanation consistent with multiple streams of research.

Realizing that there are benefits to collaboration, however, is not the same as encouraging it. Choices may depend on incentives. Thomas Kuhn was originally denied tenure, in part, because his contributions at the interface between disciplines were not considered central to any of them. The unspoken message to untenured faculty may not be to bridge disciplines but only to build from within. Information technology provides marvelous opportunities for intellectual exploration and community integration, but only if this is how people choose to use it.

Four key conclusions to draw from these observations are that the access properties of IT can lead to greater specialization if the pressure to focus exceeds the desire to explore, that incentives and growth in information can supply this pressure, and that research fragmentation resulting from specialization can potentially reduce information spillovers. Lastly, IT may give us new options but the level of community fragmentation differs by how we use it.

Reputation, Stratification, and
Winner-Take-All Markets

The creation of great quantities of information does not mean that each data point is equally valuable. One of the strongest criticisms of the "information superhighway" is that its travelers often collect a lot more dust than diamonds. In university research, the warehousing of numerous working papers, works-in-progress, and preprints exacerbates this problem. Specializing—learning the shortcuts and deciding for oneself which routes are most efficient—is one means of narrowing the routes on a roadmap thick with scenic distractions. A second strategy, however, is to choose the popular routes, to decide based on acclamation or reputation. The volume of research published each year, for example, encourages researchers to screen their readings on the basis of author and journal reputation (Stephan, 1996). For better or worse, technology plays a major role in success breeding success as reputations are picked up and broadcast to larger audiences. Through technological amplification, very modest initial differences can lead to very large subsequent differences. Consider what might happen, for example, as access to the best lecturers increases with technology. Initially, everyone attends the best lecture in their neighborhood or community and most lecturers can have roughly the same number of listeners. If remote access improves, say, through video conferencing, then slightly better lecturers can attract a majority of the listeners. With more listeners, more practice, and more feedback, the better lecturers might get better still. Figure 8.3 plots the case in which access improves from a purely local neighborhood to a completely global market. For the sake of concreteness, it assumes that there are 25 possible lectures but that bounded rationality and patience limit one's interest to no more than five lectures.

Figure 8.3 shows the probability that any one of these rank-ordered lecturers would be in a listener's local choice set as access improves. With only local access, a listener is just as likely to choose any lecturer in the neighborhood. With global access, however, only the top five lecturers have an audience. Assuming bounded rationality, broadcast technology leads to the amplification of modest differ-

FIGURE 8.3

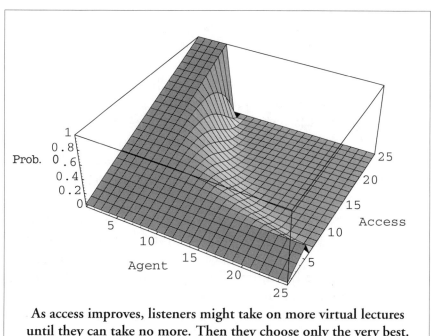

As access improves, listeners might take on more virtual lectures until they can take no more. Then they choose only the very best.

ences in reputation. Economists Frank and Cook (1995) have called this effect a "Winner-Take-All" market, and they recount observations from a story told by author Kurt Vonnegut to illustrate its effect. Consider the life of a moderately talented musician from 100 years ago. This performer might once have been a community treasure but the same person faces a life of diminished opportunity in a society that places him or her in global competition with the world's best performers. How do promising new lecturers compete with Steven J. Gould on paleontology or Peter Drucker on management? At MIT, annual presentations of Richard Feynman's posthumous lectures on physics (via videotapes) draw larger audiences than most physics classes.

The effects, however, of placing local professionals in global competition do not stop with changes in reputation. First, rising access can lead to falling affordability. Whether IT creates markets in academia, sports, or management, higher profiles can command higher prices. Second, availability can actually fall as demand rises. This occurs when broadcast options are limited but access is universal. Consider what might happen, for example, if everyone seeking financial advice had access to the private telephone number of Peter Lynch: Clogged lines might make it impossible to reach him.

This phenomenon also occurs in research. In their efforts to find collaborators, research scholars might face the same probability distribution that listeners face when choosing lectures, namely the plot in Figure 8.3. The twist is that researchers are choosing from within their own community: The source and receiver are the same, and both are boundedly rational. Although the lecturer can transfer information one-way to everyone, successful collaborators require two-way information transfers among partners. As a consequence, increased access allows researchers to aspire to their best partners, and it allows the best partners to choose one another. Once interactive collaboration begins, members may have little time for other associations. If the top researchers in Figure 8.3 choose to work with one another, the result can easily be increased stratification. Although technology access has risen, scholars outside a given partnership might judge that their colleagues' availability has actually fallen; the elite are simply too preoccupied! Telephone access can further the financial analogy. Before he became famous, Peter Lynch might have been accessible to an average investor. After his successes, however, it might take the head of Fidelity to get through.

Technology can, therefore, have the simultaneous effect of providing access to an elite scholar at the same time it places that scholar out of reach—high demand makes her inaccessible. This result is similar to that of the previous section in which IT and bounded rationality led to horizontal specialization. Here, they can lead to vertical stratification.

The main conclusions to draw from these observations are that reputations are one means of handling information overload, that broadcast IT can transform slight reputation differences into winner-take-all markets, and that IT combined with bounded rationality can lead to stratification.

INCREASED COMPETITION
VERSUS INFORMATION SHARING

The collegiality of a university depends a great deal on an open environment and on sharing information among members of its community. Yet, the degree to which community members are willing to share ideas depends significantly on interpersonal rewards. Importantly, rewards based on absolute performance encourage free exchange, while rewards based on relative performance inhibit it.

Consider two different classes with different grading policies. In one class, every student who scores above a 90 on the exam merits an A for the course. In the other class, only 10% of the students, regardless of the score distribution, will score an A. Assuming that the difficulty of the test is the same in both cases, which grading policy encourages more students to assist one another with preparation? The first policy is much more likely to encourage information sharing. It uncouples one student's grade from that of another so that one student need not do badly for another to do well. Absolute performance criteria are therefore more likely to encourage study groups since students who know slightly different material can benefit one another. Here, the point is not to comment on which policy is better: A good argument can be made that the relative policy encourages students to work harder and learn more by not collaborating on preparation. Rather, the point is to emphasize that an absolute reward policy encourages information sharing whereas a relative reward policy discourages it.

A similar distinction may affect faculty collegiality. It costs very little to share intellectual credit either through coauthorship or citation. In many ways, citing another scholar's work strengthens one's own contributions. It demonstrates familiarity with material, lays the foundation for common discourse, and outlines the research gaps one hopes to fill with new contributions. Thus, the traditional practice of scholarship is comparatively open in that it encourages sharing through dialogue and publication. Loosely speaking, authors are rewarded for their absolute performance in terms of the number and quality of their publications.

An alternate reward structure is possible which compensates not for the publication of ideas but for their economic value—a trend suggested by an increasing tendency to seek corporate research sponsorship. Sharing credit, however, is easier than sharing dollars. Possible reward structures based on the sale of information assets can have a chilling effect on dialogue. Dividing the proceeds from the sale of an idea, method, or formula is a zero sum game: The more one contributor gains, the more another contributor loses. The relative performance of each contributor must be assessed in very precise terms, creating an incentive to hoard information and deny it to others lest attribution become ambiguous. In the sharing of credit for scholarship, questions of attribution for fractions of an idea are less common. In the sharing of proceeds from a sale, attribution problems, bargaining costs, and the loss of information sharing can impose systemic costs.

The ability to sell information also depends heavily on its non-availability to the general public; if it is freely available, it is probably free. A strategy of selling information is likely to limit sharing for three reasons. First, sharing creates a second possible supplier. Bertrand, or price competition, between perfect substitutes (i.e., the same information from an alternate source) cannot sustain a market with positive prices. Second, if new research is patentable, the developer cannot legally disclose it before filing an application without risking loss of its patentability. This could introduce disclosure delays. Finally, if new research is not patentable but it has market value, it is more likely to remain a trade secret to increase its value to potential buyers or to improve the competitive status of the research sponsor. This could eliminate disclosure entirely. Evidence suggests that the privatization of information due to its high economic value is an increasingly common phenomenon. Scientific knowledge and production know-how in the form of software, genetic codes, and protein manufacturing, for example, are being patented and copyrighted at unprecedented rates (Branscombe, 1995).

Research also provides evidence that relative versus absolute reward effects of information sharing occur in industry. A study of groupware introduced into a consulting firm observed this phenomenon (Orlikowski, 1992). In a competitive up-or-out atmosphere, consultants below the level of principal would vie for a limited number of promotions largely on the basis of individual competency. Revealing unique knowledge or expertise risked shrinking any relative advantage over less qualified candidates or growing the advantage of more qualified candidates if the beneficiary did not respond with at least as much valuable information. Under the relative reward structure, competing consultants refused to share information.

Ironically, the same firm provided evidence of both absolute and relative reward systems in different contexts. At the firm's highest level, principals enjoyed permanent tenure and focused more on absolute rather than relative maximization. Their interests lay with the absolute performance of the firm and not their relative advantage over other principals. Among principals, collegiality and information sharing prevailed. Different incentives and behavior indicated the existence of their separate agendas: "Consultants feel little incentive to share their ideas for fear that they may lose status, power, and distinctive competence. Principals, on the other hand, do not share this fear and are more focused on the interests of . . . the firm than on their individual careers" (Orlikowski, 1992).

Despite the introduction of groupware technology to facilitate information sharing, it did not alter behaviors. Again, the point is that IT creates options, but preferences, uses, and choices determine results.

IMPLICATIONS : WHERE DO WE GO FROM HERE?

How then should higher education respond to the issues raised by applying theories of information and technology? The answer depends on one's purpose and whether one takes the perspective of the social planner setting educational priorities or the perspective of a single institution competing for resources. Let me conclude with three suggestions; two focus on the information asset, while the third focuses on information processing.

From the perspective of a social planner, if the purpose is to foster growth in information resources, then subsidizing education and encouraging interdisciplinary cooperation is perhaps one of few realistic solutions. The reason is that, due to its nonrival character, information exhibits "positive externalities."

In economic terms, a positive externality is a benefit to nonpartic-
ipants when a consumer engages in some transaction. Buying telephone service, for example, benefits you and the telephone company
but it also benefits friends and relatives who gain access to you even
though they bear none of your costs for service. Considering the university as an information processor, such externalities include the
social benefits of an education that a student does not consider when
paying tuition and the information spillovers that a sponsor does not
capture when buying research. Benefits falling outside pairwise transactions with a university are not received by buyers and therefore are
rarely valued. An analogy to a familiar negative externality, pollution,
will help to illustrate the nature of the social investment problem.

Pollution creates costs that we share collectively because neither
buyers nor sellers bear the costs of cleaning up. Goods that pollute are
discounted from their true price, leading buyers to overconsume
them. The opposite is true for information. If ideas spilling into the
market create benefits that we share collectively, a positive externality,
then buyers underconsume them because buyers do not profit from
ideas the rest of us use. For goods with negative externalities, a buyer
receives all the benefits for a fraction of the costs. For goods with positive externalities, a buyer pays all the costs for a fraction of the benefits. The result for universities is underconsumption, underinvest-
ment, and undervaluation. Positive externalities make research and
education prime candidates for government support.

Alternatively, if we collectively decide that public funding for
education is too expensive, then an alternate solution is to sell the
information which universities warehouse and produce. In essence,
universities might earn considerable revenue by privatizing their
information assets. This already occurs when universities charge
tuition for credit or contact hours in the classroom, that is, for information transfers. This also occurs when universities engage in technology licensing, contract research, and equity arrangements, which
are also increasingly common. Similarly, there is almost no reason
why universities ought not capture certain revenue streams currently
captured by publishers. University faculty already author, edit, review,

and purchase the journals for which publishers act largely as distribution channels. Distribution, however, offers negligible value-added in the age of the Internet.

There is a sense, however, in which the privatization of information detracts from knowledge as a public good. If universities share information in neat packages with preferred sponsors, then positive externalities decline because ideas do not diffuse as rapidly. This can also lead to information stratification in which the information rich become information richer. Presumably, anyone with valuable information can choose to exercise his knowledge in a way that gains him access to others with valuable information—an advantage which snowballs over time. Peter Lynch, for example, is likely to have much better access to knowledgeable financiers and economists than he had two decades before his investment successes. Governments need to decide whether they are as comfortable with the privatization of information and knowledge as they appear to be with the privatization of education and research; the two are closely related. For the most part, suggestions one and two are mutually exclusive alternatives. There is little reason to subsidize the privatization of information capital if subsidies are used to reduce positive externalities.

There is a third possible response to the problem of changing environments. Universities may focus on information processes rather than information products, which implies that universities need to improve their capacity for handling complex information.

One measure of information complexity is the amount of data necessary to describe the states in a system. For universities, state variables might include students, faculty, tuition, business-sponsored research, and numerous others. This information description also needs to include the relationships of numerous combinations among these variables. By most accounts, complexity, broadly interpreted, is increasing because the state variables and their relationships are changing more rapidly. Government funding priorities are different; new student constituencies are emerging among the adult population and from abroad; technology places distant colleges in local competition; and regulation has lifted mandatory retirement.

If different structures process information differently, then which ones can improve complex information processing? One that arguably handles complexity better than others is a "network organization." These are collections of cospecialized assets whose members share a common purpose and exercise joint control (Van Alstyne, 1998). Networks help flexibly cope with rising complexity and rapidly changing information.

By considering two extreme organizational forms, archetypal markets and hierarchies, we can better determine how different structures handle complexity.

A market handles complexity rather well. It matches buyers and sellers in a wide variety of possible asset combinations. In fact, the number of possible relationships is combinatorially explosive. Hypothetically, potential students, interested researchers, and available educators might each seek one another. Each could mix and match from a huge variety of combinations and secure from a pattern of private transactions what they could not find at an institution with fixed resources. The trouble with this view of a market system is that it entails huge search and coordination costs, it lacks economies of scale from specialization, and individual members have trouble establishing and maintaining reputations since transactions are rarely repeated. New combinations can flexibly emerge to handle dynamic complexity, but the amount of work to attain one is not necessarily efficient.

At the other extreme, a hierarchy assembles a specific collection of assets in order to obtain a consistent and efficient result. A central authority also tends to make decisions on behalf of the rest of the organization. This structure has limited search costs, can achieve economies of scale, and can establish credible long-term contacts. The trouble with hierarchies is that their rigid combination of assets is not very flexible and their centralized decisions often omit important decentralized information.

With respect to handling change, one important principle binds both organizational structures: The complexity of factors considered in a decision cannot exceed the complexity of the decision process. In a market, everyone decides on their optimal course of action and a combinatorial explosion of possible structures is conceivable. Complex processing ability is high. In a hierarchy, a central authority makes decisions for the organization and allocates transactions over a fixed asset combination. Complex processing ability is low. My point is not to argue that universities are hierarchies; they are neither rigidly configured nor centrally controlled. However, if a university exhibits a degree of hierarchy that is well-adapted to a given level of complexity, then a rise in complexity suggests that a more market-like structure could help process more information.

Network organizations might play this role. Their characteristics—cospecialization, common purpose, and joint control—imply higher levels of autonomy and self-sufficiency than more traditional structures. They also imply a high degree of organizational modularity as distinct from vertical integration. With a network structure, organizational boundaries are more flexible and ties to other organizations are more likely. The research on network organizations suggests that they perform better than traditional structures at managing information since this is what helps to provide members with distinctive competence. Networks also gather and process information in a distributed rather than a centralized fashion (Van Alstyne, 1998; Nohria & Eccles, 1993; Powell, 1990). They handle complexity rather well.

A number of organizations have taken this approach, from real estate ventures to fashion textiles, and from biotechnology startups to multinational chain stores. Certain nonprofit consumer advocacy groups also use network structures. This does not imply that academia should copy commercial practices; greater positive externalities, for example, skew the comparison. Still, examples are informative. Coalitions of engineering and business schools can offer programs in technological innovation superior to those offered independently. Schools of law, economics, and public policy can teach their graduates cooperatively to design regulatory mechanisms that are constitutionally sound and economically efficient. The division of labor might also be by function rather than by discipline. For example, by dividing information tasks into creation, transfer, storage, and certification, one can imagine structures that warehouse the most complete information on chemistry, but that also rank and certify individual contributions among these huge resources—a function that libraries typically do not perform. Another type of institution might have few warehoused resources but might offer unique skills in delivering the best lectures via telecommunications; thus it focuses on information transfers. Valuable partnerships, or network organizations, could then link the delivery institution with the warehousing institution or even the research institution. Network organizations combine positive attributes of other structures with some attributes of their own. Among multiple strengths, one critical skill is proving adept at the process of self-design. They adapt well in complex environments.

Certain strategies mentioned earlier also motivate the adoption of network structures, particularly modular specialization. Given the falling price of IT, recall that one strategy is to avoid IT substitutes and to emphasize IT complements. Codified, algorithmic, and rote training are aspects of education that might well pass to self-learning and IT instruction. Traditional universities enjoy no particular advantages over industry in providing efficient service in these areas (Ives & Jarvenpaa, 1996; Massy & Zemsky, 1995). Rote forms of student certification might also be handled by IT. In contrast, nonalgorithmic insight, Socratic discursive dialogue, and peer review (i.e., information certification) remain aspects of education and information exchange at which universities are unsurpassed. By lifting the geographic barriers to information exchange, IT may complement the delivery of educational services in which universities enjoy a comparative advantage even as it substitutes for those in which they do not. Pursuing IT complements argues for specializing in areas of comparative advantage, that is, aspects of creating, teaching, caching, and accrediting information that require sophisticated rather than simple processing.

Specialization appears to be the sine qua non of future success. In education as in other fields, the increased reach of IT helps create an environment in which the best drive out the merely good (Massy & Zemsky, 1995), and the winners will indeed take most if not all of these markets. The question that follows is "How specialized is specialized?" In their efforts to become world class experts on selected topics, for example, doctoral students have been known to choose theses so narrow that they sacrifice relevance for precision. Certain academic disciplines have even been criticized for being too far removed from practice. They are neither accountable nor even recountable to the general public (Cassidy, 1996).

One potentially useful guideline is to choose that level of specialization that makes one an attractive expert partner. Accountability to a partner helps ensure relevance. Complexity and change in the environment can lead the specialist in one period to become a relic in the next. Change imposes a need to balance specialized skills with more general skills in order to adapt. Partnering helps share risk, provide diverse information input, and distribute decision authority in ways that can potentially increase joint viability. In complex environments, the trick is to partner for complementary skills rather than invest in imitating the talents more expertly deployed by others. This avoids the opportunity costs associated with performing tasks at which one is second rate. Market opportunities and educational niches may themselves change and require a new partner's complementary resources in order to exploit them. In attracting partners, however, one needs to be an attractive partner. To develop a program in product innovation, for example, a first-rate business school is less likely to partner with a second-rate engineering school if the market offers better options. IT also complements network cooperation and more market-like structures because it enhances coordination (Malone, Yates, & Benjamin, 1987). The resulting cospecialization, common purpose, and coordinated control lead to network forms of organization.

CONCLUSIONS / THE BOTTOM LINE

From an institutional perspective, the greatest rewards are to be derived from anticipating the need to specialize and focusing on departments and clusters of departments that collectively provide the greatest value. In any given environment, the degree of specialization should be influenced by factors that make one an attractive partner. Too little specialization leaves a school with too little to offer. Too much specialization leaves one without much occasion to contribute. A more complex environment implies a need for more partners and more resource coordination. This implies specializing within disciplines and information roles, and balancing specialization with complementary partnerships and resources. To a university, it also implies providing departments with greater autonomy and the ability to seek complementary resources outside the core institutional structure. Information processing pressures suggest a move toward network structures.

Given the university's role in creating, teaching, caching, and accrediting information, educators can benefit significantly by applying a model of the university as an information processor to their strategic thinking. Such a model captures the public good versus private capital tradeoff and recognizes the tension between rewarding information sharing versus rewarding information sales. It also provides important insights into evolving phenomena including specialization, fragmentation, incentive competition, winner-take-all markets, and intensification of reputations. Using this framework also suggests how increasingly rapid changes in the environment can increase the need for improved information processing capacity.

As information complexity rises, our colleges and universities will need to adapt even as they continue to play an essential role in shaping our information institutions. Half the information challenge is to predict the consequences of information pressures. Then, given that no future scenario is inevitable, the other half is to seek such leverage as can lead to the futures we want. The only real tragedy would be to treat these trends as inescapable. Information and technology create opportunity—they give us new choices with which to seek the more attractive futures, and avoid the less attractive alternatives.

REFERENCES

Alvarez, L. W., et al. (1980). Extraterrestrial cause for the cretaceous-tertiary extinction: Experimental results and theoretical interpretation. *Science,* 208 (4448), 1095-1108.

Black, F., & Scholes, M. (1973). The pricing of options and corporate liabilities. *Journal of Political Economy,* 81 (3), 637-654.

Branscombe, A. W. (1995). *Who owns information?* Cambridge, MA: MIT Press.

Brynjolfsson, E. (1993). The productivity paradox of information technology. *Communications of the ACM,* 96 (12), 67-77.

Cassidy, J. (1996, December 2). Department of disputation: The decline of economics. *The New Yorker,* 50.

Cummings, A., et al. (1992). *University libraries and scholarly communication.* Washington, DC: Association of Research Libraries.

Frank, R. H., & Cook, P. J. (1995). *The winner-take-all society.* New York, NY: Free Press.

Gaspar, J., & Glaeser, E. L. (1996, May). *Information technology and the future of cities.* National Bureau of Economics Research, 5562.

Hoffman, C. (1995, November). *Federal support for education, fiscal years 1980 to 1995.* Washington, DC: US Government Printing Office.

Ives, B., & Jarvenpaa, S. (1996, Spring). Will the Internet revolutionize business education and research? *Sloan Management Review,* 33-42.

Kaufer, D. S., & Carley, K. M. (1993). *Communication at a distance: The influence of print on sociocultural organization and change.* Hillsdale, NJ: Lawrence Erlbaum Associates.

Krugman, P., (1996). White collars turn blue. *New York Times Magazine,* 199, 106-107.

Kuhn, T. (1970). *The structure of scientific revolutions* (2nd ed.). Chicago, IL: University of Chicago Press.

Lenzner, R., & Johnson, S. S. (1997). Seeing things as they are. *Forbes, 39*.

Leslie, J. (1995). Mail bonding. *Wired, 2* (3), 42-48.

Malone, T. W., Yates, J., & Benjamin, R. I. (1987). Electronic markets and electronic hierarchies. *Communications of the ACM, 30* (6), 484-497.

Massy, W. F., & Zemsky, R. (1995, June). Using information technology to enhance academic productivity. *National Learning Infrastructure Initiative*.

McLuhan, M., & Powers, B. R. (1989). *The global village: Transformations in world life and media in the 21st century*. New York, NY: Oxford University Press.

Moffat, A. S. (1993, February 26). New meetings tackle the knowledge conundrum. *Science, 259*, 1253-55.

Noam, E. (1995, October 13). Electronics and the dim future of the university. *Science, 270*, 247-249.

Nohria, N., & Eccles, R. C. (Eds.). (1993). *Networks and organizations*. Boston, MA: Harvard Business School Press.

Orlikowski, W. (1992). Learning from notes: Organizational issues in groupware implementation. *Proceedings of the Conference on Computer Supported Cooperative Work* (CSCW). Toronto, Canada: ACM.

Pool, I. d. S. (1983). Tracking the flow of information. *Science, 221* (4611), 609-613.

Powell, W. W. (Ed.). (1990). Neither market nor hierarchy: Network forms of organization. In B. M. Staw & L. L. Cummings (Eds.), *Research in organizational behavior*, Vol. 12. Greenwich, CT: JAI Press.

Quinn, J. B. (1992). *Intelligent enterprise*. New York, NY: Free Press.

Romer, P. (1986). Increasing returns and long run growth. *Journal of Political Economy*, 94 (5), 1002-1037.

Romer, P. (1990). Endogenous technological change. *Journal of Political Economy,* 98 (5), S71-S102.

Rowe, K. (1996, April 3). At conference, Dertouzos discusses links to the past. *MIT Tech Talk,* 4.

Saxenian, A. (1994). Lessons from Silicon Valley. *Technology Review,* 97 (5), 42-51.

Simon, H. (1973). Applying information technology to organizational design. *Public Administration Review,* 268-278.

Simon, H.A. (1957). *Models of man.* New York, NY: John Wiley & Sons.

Sproull, L., & Kiesler, S. (1991). *Connections: New ways of working in the networked organization.* Cambridge, MA: MIT Press.

Stephan, P. E. (1996). The economics of science. *Journal of Economic Literature,* 34 (4), 1199-1235.

Van Alstyne, M. W. (1998). The state of network organization: A survey in three frameworks. *Journal of Organizational Computing and Electronic Commerce,* 7 (3), 83-151.

Van Alstyne, M. W., & Brynjolfsson, E. (1995). *Communication networks and the rise of an information elite: Do computers help the rich get richer?* Amsterdam: International Conference on Information Systems.

ACKNOWLEDGMENTS

This article is based on a talk presented at the Stanford Forum for Higher Education futures whose participants greatly strengthened the ideas presented. Since the talk drew heavily on two existing research papers, a significant intellectual debt is owed to Erik Brynjolfsson who coauthored the original work on Internet economics. Ideas on complex organizations have also benefited from discussions with Yaneer Bar-Yam. Others whose insights have improved various drafts include Carol Frances, Pamela Gann, Robert Laubacher, Bill Massy, Joel Meyerson, Jim Orlin, and Jerry Prothero. Any remaining errors are certainly mine.

The Unsustainability of Traditional Libraries

Brian L. Hawkins

Libraries are at the very center of those characteristics that define a society. Benjamin Franklin, understanding that free and open access to recorded knowledge is the intellectual foundation of a democratic society and free market economy, created the first public library in Philadelphia at the turn of the 19th century.

At the turn of the 20th century, Andrew Carnegie of Pittsburgh created Carnegie Libraries in communities across the country—public libraries that gave ordinary citizens the access to knowledge and the benefits of scientific research previously enjoyed only by the elite. The Carnegie Libraries grew into the system of school libraries, public libraries, and research libraries that generations of immigrants would use as a road to upward mobility, inventors would use to create new businesses, and teachers and students would use to pursue their scholarly endeavors.

But as the beginning of the 21st century approaches, the very survival of our libraries is seriously threatened. While the electronic superhighway promises vast amounts of information available in an almost ubiquitous fashion, economic and technological forces are narrowing our citizens' access to information. School libraries are closing all over the country, public libraries are cutting hours, and research libraries are cutting subscriptions to journals and library materials at an alarming rate.

As great as the economic threats to libraries are, however, perhaps the greater threat is the perception that technology will solve these problems, and that all someone has to do is search the World Wide Web for any information one needs. A vast amount of information is indeed available on the web today, but it is not a coherent collection of information. In addition, the amount of scholarly, intellectual, and aesthetic information is truly minimal, and access to the web is anything but egalitarian. These are a few of the concerns that must be communicated clearly and articulately to our college presidents and provosts.

It is not surprising that people have come to believe that the digital library is already well toward completion. We see television commercials suggesting that a student in Italy completed a doctoral dissertation by using digital resources via the library at the University of Indiana. What people fail to realize is that these important experiments are enormously costly, not systematic, and are not sustainable without special philanthropic and corporate support. Digitization of library materials is not happening en masse, nor is it likely to with each institution continuing to act independently. Contrary to apparent popular opinion, we are not making significant strides in making library materials available electronically, and our current efforts are best characterized as experimental, episodic, and uncoordinated. In the meantime, we are rapidly losing financial capacity to support traditional library collections.

At a series of meetings held in 1994, chief academic officers and librarians from many of our greatest institutions of higher education gathered to share their thoughts on the future of research libraries. Most envision a future with universal access, by students and faculty, to information in all possible media via a single, multifunction workstation. This vision is shared by our universities' technology leaders, as well as by many faculty who anticipate new and exciting methods of instruction allowing students to integrate the knowledge of the ages. These conferences, however, also found another commonality, "that of not having any plan or vision on how we might achieve this dream and get from here to there!" (Dougherty & Hughes, 1991).

Academic leaders, librarians, and technologists all seem to be waiting for the information revolution to arrive, apparently believing it is just around the corner because they keep hearing about it on television and reading about it in the press. We will not see this wonderful future, however, unless we focus on how to create it. If we do not begin immediately, our libraries, our educational institutions, and indeed the very intellectual fiber of our broader society could be in jeopardy.

For the last two decades, librarians have warned us of the "slow fires" within the walls of our libraries—the acid within the paper destroying the books that represent the intellectual and cultural history of our civilization. Despite the seriousness of this problem, it is minor when compared with the potentially crippling economic threats to the ability of our libraries to store and preserve information. There have been cries of warning regarding the erosion of our libraries' ability to acquire information due to inflationary trends, but the full impact does not seem to have been fully recognized.

In the 15-year period from 1981 to 1995, the library acquisition budgets of 89 of the nation's finest schools nearly tripled, and in real dollars increased by an average of 82% when corrected for inflation, using the Consumer Price Index (CPI). These increases may seem impressive, and they represent major commitments on the part of these universities, but the reality is that the average library in this elite group of libraries lost 38% of its buying power during this period, as shown in Figure 9.1 (Stubbs & Molyneux, 1990; Stubbs, 1992). In those 15 years, the inflation rate for acquisitions was consistently in the mid-teens. Although the costs of books and monographs did not rise quite as fast, the cost of some serials—especially those in the sciences—increased over 20% a year. If these trends continue, by the year 2030 the acquisitions budgets of our finest libraries will have only 20% of the buying power they had just 50 years earlier.

FIGURE 9.1

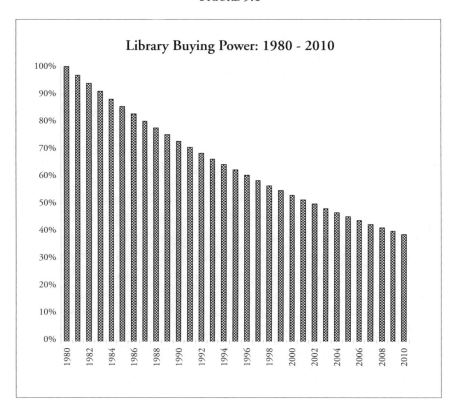

Library Buying Power: 1980 - 2010

This problem is universal in scope, but the solution has been relegated largely to research institutions because historically they have developed the largest, most complex, and oldest collections. The 89 schools that were analyzed represent nearly 40% of all library acquisitions among the more than 3,200 colleges and universities in this country. The research universities of this country have assumed a major societal role in creating, preserving, and organizing the world's knowledge, and have been funded through student tuition, through formula-funding at public institutions, and through endowed book funds. Our great universities are losing their library buying power, and none of these historical sources of revenue can keep up with the increases in cost.

As dire as these projections may be, it should be recognized that they are based on the precarious assumption that library acquisition budgets will increase an average of 8% compounded per year as they have for the past 15 years. This amount is nearly three times inflation, and nearly twice the amount of total increases in the cost of higher education. With the pressures on higher education to cut costs even more, the problem of sustaining our libraries is probably even worse than just predicted. Recognizing that there is no way for the old paradigm to work, we must address these problems immediately. A recent Mellon Foundation report reached the same conclusion:

> The rapidly rising prices of materials, the continued increase in the number of items available for purchase, the fact that university libraries seem to be acquiring a declining share of the world's output, the impracticality of continuing to build large, costly, warehouse-type structures to shelve printed materials, thus replicating collections that exist elsewhere— these and other developments cause one to ask whether established practices, which are already eroding, can be continued for very much longer (Cummings et al., 1992).

Libraries clearly will not scale into the 21st century using the current model. We must develop a new paradigm that meets the economic parameters of our institutions, and yet still supports the traditional values of libraries and scholarship. While the economic problems are significant, we should not focus on this dilemma solely as a financial problem. The problem of long-term access to information, and the extent to which the scholarly record is being lost, should worry anyone concerned about the future of the university. Traditionally, libraries collect only about 6% of all information that is published. Without intervention, even this amount of preservation is in serious jeopardy.

There are three basic contributors to the total cost of a library: purchase or acquisition costs, personnel costs, and space costs, each of which needs to be explored to fully appreciate why the traditional library cannot be sustained as it has in the past.

PURCHASE COSTS

Librarians and others concerned about the library collections in colleges and universities have focused on acquisition costs. The extraordinary impact of inflationary increases in the 1980s and 1990s, especially on scientific, technical, and medical journals, has been well documented, and was illustrated in the earlier graph related to library buying power. Acquisition budgets have outstripped inflation significantly, but have fallen far short of the increase in total acquisition costs of materials, shown in Figure 9.2 as increasing at 12% compounded. The earlier chart showing the decrease in buying power was the result of an earlier analysis based on data from 1981 through 1991. In looking at Figure 9.2, however, one sees that the gap between the 12% increase in materials cost and the average increase in Association of Research Libraries (ARL) acquisitions budgets increases at a faster rate beginning in 1990, as the slope of the line for ARL acquisition budgets begins to flatten out.

This reduction in the increase of ARL budgets reflects the broader economic pressures facing higher education. Throughout the 1990s, our universities have been pressured to control costs and increase accountability. The average increase in the average total library budget and the average acquisition budget declined dramatically during the five-year period from 1991 to 1995, as shown in Table 9.1. If the average library acquisition budget is maintained at the levels of the last five years, then the degradation in the ability to acquire information speeds up. If similar levels are maintained in the future, the projection made earlier—that buying power in 2030 will be just 20% of that in 1981—appears overly optimistic. The 20% level would be reached much sooner—23 years earlier—in 2007.

FIGURE 9.2

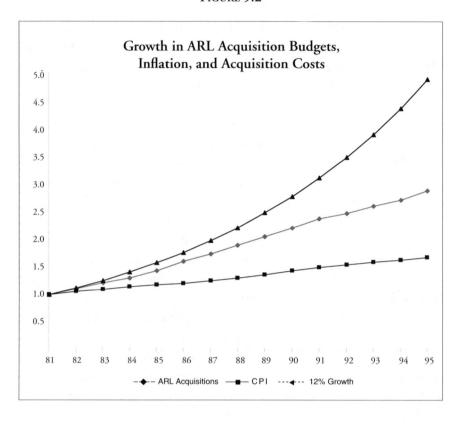

TABLE 9.1

**Average Increases in Total Library Budgets
and Acquisition Budgets by Five-Year Segments**

	1981-85	1986-90	1991-95
Total Budget	9.25%	7.52%	4.1%
Acquisitions	9.67%	8.98%	5.4%

FIGURE 9.3

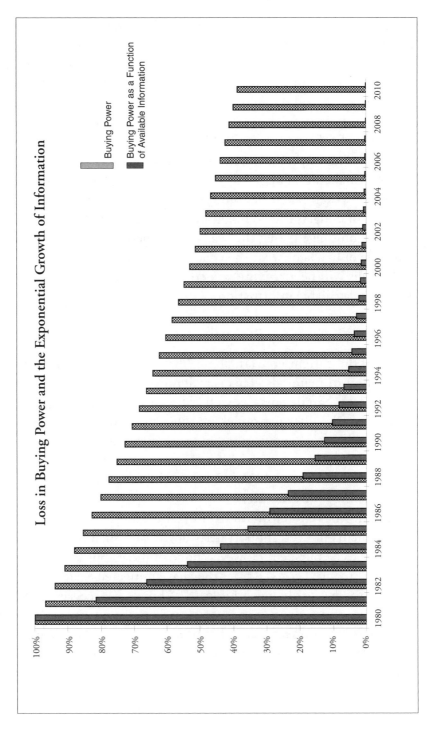

Loss in Buying Power and the Exponential Growth of Information

Exacerbating the declining growth in purchasing power is the rapidly increasing rate of available information. Many experts believe the information explosion is well underway, with information doubling every two to three years. The amount of published information that is available and desirable for a library may be increasing at a lesser rate, but information growth is a real issue in the acquisition of library materials. If information is doubling every four years, then there is a compounding impact of inflation and information growth. In 1981, it was estimated that about 6% of the then available information was collected. When taken in combination, as shown in Figure 9.3, the decrease in budgets due to inflation and the projected increase in total information suggests that the available budgets in 2001 will be able to purchase only 2% of what they had 20 years before. This implies that collections will be archiving something of the order of one-tenth of 1% of the available information.

PERSONNEL COSTS

Much of the current concern about library costs focuses on the initial acquisition of materials. This is a significant problem, but there are other less apparent costs as well. The cost of catalogers, reference librarians, and other personnel are substantial, averaging about twice the annual cost of acquisitions in the typical research library in the United States. However, without these talented support and service providers, a library would only be a warehouse, and not a vital part of the academic infrastructure.

Strides have been made to develop cooperative and sharing arrangements to keep support costs down, and such solutions should continue to be pursued. However, none of these approaches have substantively reduced costs. Rather they have mitigated against losing services in the face of reduced budgets. While it is necessary to further collaborate and cooperate in leveraging specialist talents of catalogers, etc., the two-to-one nature of support costs to actual acquisitions reflects the labor intensive nature of libraries. This is not surprising as libraries have long been known for their commitments to service and support of students and faculty. Jaroslav Pelikan (1992) in describing the role of the library in meeting the broad missions of the university, suggests that:

> As the volume of scholarly helps increases, the need for professional guidance in the use of such helps increases with it; and that professional guidance can come only from subject bibliographers who are sensitive and thoroughly trained and whom research scholars recognize as their peers and colleagues in the raising up of future scholars.

Despite the obvious importance of reference librarians, it is unlikely we will see the employment of such professionals increase proportionately with the growth of patrons, much less with the growth of information. In fact, the percentage of budgets spent on operations decreased from an average of over 67% of the typical library budget to nearly 63%, as shown in Figure 9.4.

FIGURE 9.4

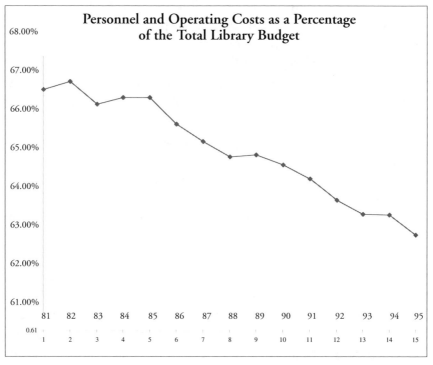

This decrease has two causes. The first is the effort to keep up with the inflationary spiral of costs associated with acquisitions. This is seen in Figure 9.5, which shows the percentage increase in total budget and the two elements that comprise this total—acquisitions and operations. The rate of operational increases is clearly smaller. The second reason for the decrease is that the last five years of this period have been characterized by significant reductions in university budgets, and the support staffs of libraries were not exempted from these reductions. While information was growing and attempts to reengineer the support structures of our universities were underway, the ratios changed only slightly. Although the trend is in the "right" direction in leveraging available resources, Pelikan and others would argue it is in the wrong direction in support of scholarship.

As the information explosion continues, and as more and more information is available, everyone will need more help finding, sorting, and filtering the available materials. The number of users, the amount of information, and the costs of a labor-intensive model clearly make the current model unfeasible and unscalable.

While libraries may be able to share or pool technical support services, it is unlikely they can significantly increase the efficiency of personnel who support users directly. A "virtual reference librarian" supporting many users on a network may gain some leverage someday, but the increasing numbers of users coupled with the current lack of resources are a growing concern in the short term.

It is unreasonable to expect any significant transformation soon in the way libraries assist their users to sort and select information because the issues of "filtering" become greater as the amount of available information increases. Some place high hope in the ongoing development of "agents" or "knowbots" to electronically filter through the increasing mass of available information, selecting the precise information that matches a person's individual profile of interests and preferences. While dreams of these "digital aliens" are intriguing, a prudent planner should expect increases—not decreases—in the human capital needed to help people navigate the network, at least in the near term. In this environment of increased access and availability of networked information, eliminating unnecessary and irrelevant information will prove to be a larger challenge than finding it.

FIGURE 9.5

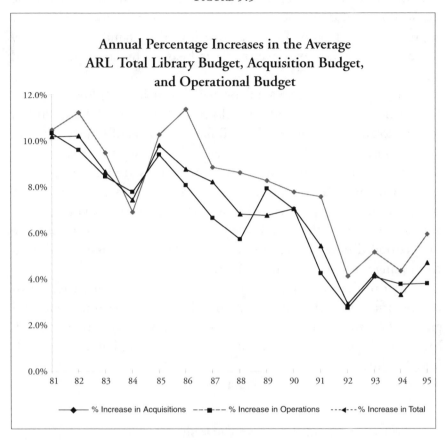

SPACE COSTS

While the problems associated with the acquisition of new information are alarming, focusing on this set of costs masks the magnitude of the real problem. If we proceed with the library model as we have known it, the costs associated with storing and archiving the information will bankrupt our institutions of higher education.

This problem was clearly identified 20 years ago, but our institutions failed to heed the warnings (Gore, 1976). If one assumes that new building costs are approximately $170 per square foot, then the cost of physically housing a single volume approaches $20, which would correspond with the $10 to $12 cost identified in 1982 if inflation is factored in (Leighton & Weber, 1986). This figure was corroborated in another study (Getz, 1994). In addition to the physical cost of constructing this space, it costs Brown University approximately $1 per volume per year for maintenance of the library building, counting expenses such as heat, light, air control, and custodial service.

Looking at the experience at Brown University, building construction in the last three decades would be in excess of $60,000,000 in today's dollars. In addition, the maintenance costs of library facilities at Brown exceed $2,000,000 per year. Often these associated costs of housing and maintaining our library collections are ignored because space costs often are not reflected in line items that appear in the library budget. Regardless of where they appear, however, these annual costs—plus the capital costs of new construction—need to be understood if one is to appreciate the level of crisis associated with continuing our current library traditions.

The problem is apparent if we look at library construction in combination with the size of the total library collection. Figure 9.6 graphs the size of the Brown University library collection. The black bars represent the construction of a new library or opening a new dedicated facility.

Figure 9.6

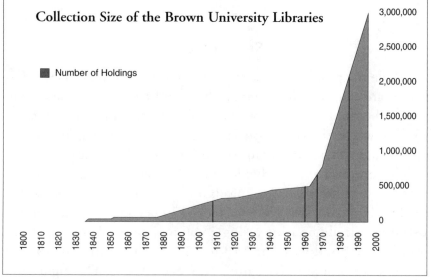

The three libraries built at Brown since 1961 reflect an addition of over 200,000 square feet of space and a very large proportion of all new construction that occurred at the university in the past three decades. With the information explosion occurring in the exponential fashion already described, the cost of physically housing these materials will become astronomical.

This problem is duplicated to some greater or lesser degree on every campus in the United States, as well as on campuses around the world. This is especially disturbing when one takes into consideration the conventional wisdom that only 10% of the collection is heavily used, while 90% of the collection is used infrequently, and the vast majority of the collection never circulates. To be sure, circulation does not directly correlate with use or with the value that access to these materials might have. Access to information, no matter how often it circulates, is a strongly held value that is part of the fundamental mission of a library—especially a research library. Still, the old model of access cannot be sustained, and should not be duplicated by scores of other institutions.

In keeping with the "efficiency" value of the corporate world of the past decade, libraries have been criticized for not adopting a "just in time" model of information (vis-à-vis the industrial manufacturing model), but instead maintaining a "just in case" philosophy. While this parallel phraseology is perhaps clever in the criticism of the failure to achieve efficiency, what is missed is that the archival and stewardship roles of the library are essential to the enhancement of knowledge and cannot be judged solely by a criterion of efficiency. Certainly the efficiency of the archival function can—and should be—enhanced, but the archiving of important information is extremely important to scholarship and to our society "just in case" it might be needed by scholars and practitioners in years to come.

It is abundantly clear, with the dramatic decrease in the price performance curve of electronic information storage, that reductions in the cost of storing information could be achieved if electronic storage were the accepted medium for archiving scholarly information. Not only would electronic storage be far cheaper, it would also eliminate the present duplication. Information could be available in a very few defined locations on the network, and yet accessible to users internationally, at all times and places that the network was available. This aspect of the cost of scholarly information is the most easily dealt with. It draws upon a solution that requires no new innovation and which attains the needed increases in efficiency.

Moving toward a cooperative strategy of electronic storage will not only reduce problems associated with physical space, but will also address the critical problems of preservation of print materials that libraries are facing. The decaying materials, which are being destroyed by the acid-based paper upon which they were printed, must be either treated, copied, or stored on an alternative medium if they are to be saved. Movement of many of our library resources to an electronic medium would solve multiple problems, although in all likelihood, new and unanticipated challenges will emerge in connection with this new paradigm.

FUTURE DIRECTIONS IN SUPPORTING LIBRARIES

Clearly, in the current economic context with unprecedented pressures on higher education to slow the increase in tuition, dramatic increases in library budgets are unreasonable to expect. However, if the solution to making up this gap is not adding money at an exponential rate, then what can be done? The following steps should be considered as part of a broad strategy.

Enlist Faculty Support for a New Paradigm

At present, our colleges and universities subsidize and pay the costs of research. The faculty then give this intellectual property away to professional organizations and profit-making publishers, only to have the colleges and universities buy this material back at ever increasing prices. In the long term, this model will devastate the scholarly publication paradigm. Part of the solution is to have professional organizations and other nonprofit organizations become their own publishers and distribute their materials electronically over the network. If scholars become their own publishers, and if these materials are contributed to a "commons," then a sustainable model begins to emerge

(Okerson, 1992). The most fundamental change that must occur is the way in which rights are given to publishers for the academic information generated within the higher education community. This basic premise is not new, but it is becoming of greater and greater importance, and is well summarized in the Mellon Report.

> Alternatives to current copyright management can be imagined. For example, universities could claim joint ownership of scholarly writings with the faculty they pay to produce them, then prohibit unconditional assignment to third parties, thus becoming important players in the publishing business themselves. Or universities could request that faculty members first submit manuscripts to publishers whose pricing policies are more consonant with larger educational objectives. Another possibility is that university-negotiated licenses grant unlimited copying to libraries and individual scholars and specify said permission in the copyright statement. All these proposals are extensions of the broader idea under current discussion, that universities should reclaim some responsibility for disseminating the results of faculty scholarship (Cummings et al., 1992).

The authors of the Mellon Report go further to suggest that in an electronic world at least some of the functions of publishers could be avoided if the faculty editorial and review efforts become part of the "circle of gifts" that fuel such an enterprise. Just the act of giving limited permissions and retaining the copyright preserves the right to freely disseminate information and begins to address this massive problem. An active effort must be mounted to stop current practices of giving away exclusive rights to the developments that come from our institutions of higher education.

To enlist the support of faculty, we must educate them about these issues, and advocate their support to publish with those groups who are most consonant with the broader set of academic values. Recently, at the University of Wisconsin, a faculty resolution was passed, urging faculty members to:

... consider publishing work with publishers whose interests are sympathetic to the academic enterprise. University presses and scholarly societies offer avenues for the dissemination of information that remain under the control of the academic community. The university should continue to support and encourage those institutions whose function is to make the results of research available on a nonprofit basis (University of Wisconsin faculty, 1996).

Of all of the suggestions made here, this change in the scholarly communication paradigm is the singular most essential change in creating a sustainable model for research libraries.

Develop a New Paradigm

What is needed is a collection of information, in many formats, stored electronically in locations throughout the world, but organized, collected, and shared via a central networked organization. It would be a library that draws upon a myriad of resources that already exist, and supplemented with donations and purchases of intellectual property through a radically new business model that could reverse—or at least slow—the devastating economic decline destroying our great libraries.

Much of the private and public sector has been challenged to reengineer practices that were designed for the industrial age, but which are ineffective and cumbersome as we make the transition into an information age. Libraries are no exception. Our industrial age libraries are not scaleable into the next century, into an information age. If one believes that the intellectual and information legacy of our civilization must be preserved, then a revolutionary solution is in order. However, as suggested by Harvard University's head librarian, technology alone will not solve this problem:

> The greatest challenge facing library leaders in the next decade is not to implement new technology, it is to implement new entrepreneurially oriented management structures and cultures in our ailing industrial age libraries (DeGennaro, 1990).

A commonly discussed solution to these problems is to move to an electronic model where information access—rather than ownership—is the defining characteristic of a quality library. Because of the "shareable" nature of information as described by Harlan Cleveland (1982), existing library resources could be leveraged if the same access to information were assured and the abundant duplication of purchases that characterizes the present system were eliminated. This access model has been widely accepted as the future to which institutions should aspire. It suggests economies of scale in buying the rights to use information as needed, rather than purchasing it with the notion that someone might someday have use for it.

How does one define a collection policy in an electronic environment? Historically, a college or university defined its collections as a function of the academic programs that it offered. In this nonduplicative world, a new business model needs to be found that looks at information from a broader and more centralized approach. Such a model is described in some detail elsewhere (Hawkins, 1994), and this or some other more centralized and less fractionated solution is critical. But while a more centralized effort is called for, it cannot and should not be a single entity for a number of reasons. This philosophy is best expressed in the philosophy underpinning the National Digital Library Federation, which may be the embryo of such an effort.

As the nation's cultural resources become increasingly represented in digital form, the need grows to collect, preserve, and provide broad access to those resources in ways that are both efficient and affordable. The concept of building a national digital library captures our aspiration to meet this growing need. However, we cannot expect any single institution to serve as the repository for the nation's cultural resources in digital form. Nor, if we posit a system of independent, distributed repositories, can we expect them to manage to standards of broad accessibility, efficiency, and affordability without also positing a level of collective action. The National Digital Library Federation aims to define, promote, and encourage the development of the necessary means for the nation's digital libraries to act collectively and bring together, or "federate" in the national interest the digital heritage which they manage (Planning Task Force, 1996).

This kind of federated approach is essential to capture the existing strengths of our nation's greatest libraries, and yet to move to a more centralized and common solution which is so essential if we are to renew and reinvent the American library tradition for the high technology society of the 21st century.

Use Electronic Distribution

Distribution of information over the network is one of the keys to cost reduction. The work that has been done so far, however, suggests that the savings in paper, binding, mail distribution, etc. do not appear to be as great as one imagines. There are still labor-intensive processes of editorial review and peer review, copyediting, and production preparation embedded in the process. While some advocates suggest that some of these functions can be reduced or eliminated in an electronic world, clearly the quality of scholarly publication would change. Professionals in specific fields must be the judge as to whether these changes would be deleterious. The added value of these processes, however, will certainly come under greater scrutiny. Although current work suggests that the savings inherent in electronic distribution might be only 35%, these analyses fail to consider the "downstream" costs of support and storage.

Distributing information over the network fundamentally changes the library model. In the model that has been operative since Alexandria, scholars have been required to go to the library, and its resources were limited to those who could get there, while the new library is brought to the scholar. This more egalitarian access has the strong potential of increasing the volume of information—or at least the volume of scholarly "products"—being generated in a scholarly publishing environment.

Lobby for Appropriate Copyright Policy

Further changes in copyright law as it applies to the electronic world must be explored. Many aspects of information in an electronic world need review, including the concept of fair use, the contributions and availability of information in the public domain, and the need to balance personal gain and societal cost. As national and global information infrastructures are being established, it is imperative that public policy issues be carefully discussed. We must assure that the newly created laws, regulations, and other restrictions keep the public interest and the availability of general information clearly in focus.

Explore New Sources of Revenue

No library has ever been "free" in that there were no costs associated with it, but in an ideal world there would be no charges directly assessed to the patron or end user. While this principle makes it very difficult to define a feasible business plan, it is essential to creating the kind of egalitarian and democratic academic environment to which we must aspire. The very nature of the democratic process assumes a free flow of information, an informed populace, and an environment in which the marketplace of ideas determines truth. This basic premise is central to Jeffersonian democracy, and there is no reason to move away from the model of the free library just because the economics of a paper environment are becoming untenable, or because we shift the medium on which we store our words.

The costs of most of the world's great libraries have been borne by tuition paid by students, gifts from philanthropists, taxes paid by citizens, or a combination of all three. As has already been suggested, the ability to enhance or even sustain the revenues from these sources is questionable. Furthermore, many users of these library resources have never "paid" for this free access. If we are able to move away from the model of the self-contained library, with various stakeholders contributing to a "commons" that is available electronically, then a new model for revenues might emerge. In such an environment, the burden of financing libraries could be shared among institutions of higher education, public libraries, K-12 systems, corporations, the federal government, international partners, and philanthropic groups. It is important to involve all stakeholders in this process—and to avoid a pay-per-view model of libraries—to maintain the traditional values that are so important to our educational systems and our society at large. These values have the potential of being endangered if commercial interests drive this new paradigm.

ACADEMIC OPPORTUNITIES

This paper has focused on the economic crisis facing the traditional library and possible solutions. It should be stressed, however, that these proposed changes also offer exciting new academic opportunities that should not be overlooked in the attempt to address the economic problems.

New Types of Scholarship

There are many advantages to having information available in an electronic format, and it could change the nature of scholarship. Electronic distribution allows for the integration of information as well as its retrieval. With the availability of electronic information, software can assist the user in locating information more easily, information can be integrated and connected to related concepts, and compound documents incorporating text, pictures, video, and sound can allow for multimedia environments that create new educational horizons. The recognition that the amount of information in our society is becoming overwhelming, and that we need new tools to navigate this information is not new. More than 50 years ago, Vannevar Bush, Franklin Roosevelt's science adviser, stated:

> The difficulty seems to be not so much that we publish unduly in view of the extent and variety of present-day interests, but rather that publication has extended far beyond our present ability to make real use of the record. The summation of human experience is being expanded at a prodigious rate, and the means we use for threading through the consequent maze to the momentarily important item is the same as was used in the days of square-rigged ships (Bush, 1945).

Today's technology gives us many tools to navigate this morass of information, many of them based upon Bush's concept of facilitating the reader in working his or her way through this process. While much of the technology and software needed to help people navigate through large amounts of information has been developed, there has not been corresponding movement in making the informational resources of our society available in an electronic format.

With an electronic library a whole new dimension of scholarship and education will emerge. Text stored electronically permits scholars to quickly search enormous amounts of information, and to ask new questions that would have been impossible to address with text in printed form. This "new information" will undoubtedly include hypertextual materials, with finding aids embedded in the text. It will include compound documents including images, data sets, graphics, and other multimedia materials, which have the potential of profoundly affecting the ways in which students are educated, and in which scholarship is shared.

More Integrative Approaches to Thinking

The vast amounts of information that we encounter can be bewildering. The information explosion is causing greater and greater difficulty in keeping up with material in one's field, much less learning how different areas of scholarship intersect and affect one another. While our scholarship is becoming more specialized, it is making the process of integrative learning—one of the key goals of a liberally educated person—even more difficult. Marshall McLuhan, the communication philosopher, suggested that as the new medium of television and global telecommunications emerged, we would become a "global village." Instead, with electronic networks and with greater emphasis on specialization we face the danger of allowing thousands of tiny global villages to emerge, none of which is particularly connected to the others. We need to create educational environments that are interdisciplinary in nature, and which show how concepts link to other areas—to the architectural influences, the musical trends, or the political themes that are associated with some historical period or phenomenon.

These "linkages" can be embedded into information that is stored electronically, thus allowing a person to peruse these related topics, not with the commitment of months in the stacks of a great library, but with the push of a button. This "linking" software is critical if we are to prepare liberally educated persons who must cope with lateral integration of information as well as vertical specialization. However, it takes the availability of electronic information, and specialized software, to make this dream come true, and to address the concerns expressed by Harlan Cleveland.

> It is an open secret that the modern university is not well suited to the task of educating people for the get-it-all-together function. The university's self-image, its organization, and its reward systems all tilt against breadth.... The more we learn, ironically, the less tied together is our learning. It's not situation-as-a-whole thinking, it's the separation of specialized kinds of knowledge ... (Cleveland, 1985).

More Opportunity in Support of Lifelong Learning

It is ever more clear that education cannot be something that is accomplished exclusively at the front end of one's life. Learning must be a lifelong process, and the opportunities to pursue education must be ever more available wherever a person might be. Whether that distance is measured in physical miles or psychological miles—in the north woods of Maine, for example, or the long mile from the New York Public Library to a tenement in Brooklyn—if we don't try and create an information infrastructure that is technically and electronically available to everyone, we will miss an important opportunity to improve our society.

With an electronic library, a person's rural or metropolitan residence would not affect his or her ability to access the scholarly works, new scientific advances, or artistic performances stored in such an entity. This resource would mitigate the further polarization in our society of those who have books in one's home and those who do not.

> Both the processing and the uses of information are undergoing an unprecedented technological revolution. Not only are machines now able to deal with many kinds of information at high speed and in large quantities, but it is also possible to manipulate these quantities so as to benefit from them in new ways. This is perhaps nowhere truer than in the field of education. One can predict that in a few more years millions of schoolchildren will have access to what Philip of Macedon's

son Alexander enjoyed as a royal prerogative: the services of a tutor as well-informed and as responsive as Aristotle (Suppes, 1966).

CONCLUSION

It is clear that the current unit of analysis—the campus library—cannot survive in the existing environment. The leveraging of library resources is clearly called for, with the best solution being at the largest system-level possible—an international group of cooperating libraries. While associations of campuses, consortia, and other groupings will alleviate the problem, the best solution is found when no system or national boundaries are limiting factors, but where information is maximally available. This principle is already shown to be the case in one of the few present examples of information that is available across virtually all existing boundaries.

> For the sake of science, the knowledge base of molecular biology should be a public, international electronic library, supported by all for the benefit of all. No one organization or nation should control this type of information for public gain. Another reason for public ownership, especially of scientific knowledge, is that database and knowledge management is of such magnitude that individuals and their organizations cannot be expected to bear this burden as they have in the past (Matheson, 1988).

This illustrates the intellectual advantages as well as the economic advantages of a broader system. While there may be a sense of nostalgia for the self-contained library on campus, it is a luxury that is no longer affordable economically or intellectually if our libraries and educational systems are to survive.

It is fine to suggest that the solution to the problems of the library rest in looking across system boundaries, but the competitive instincts of our campus cultures currently work against this. Status is conferred upon an academic institution for having more volumes in its library than that of a competing institution. We rank the "best" libraries as a

function of the total number of holdings, rather than the appropriate-
ness of the collection in service of curricula, the quality of services, or
other qualitative measures. Part of the reason higher education finds
itself in this difficult situation with respect to its libraries is a long and
unproductive history of competition rather than cooperation. The
new electronic library would be a major step in reversing these tendencies and overcoming some of the inherent difficulties identified by
Patricia Battin several years ago.

> Commitment to new cooperative interinstitutional mecha-
> nisms for sharing infrastructure costs—such as networks,
> print collections, and database development and access—in
> the recognition that continuing to view information tech-
> nologies and services as a bargaining chip in the competition
> for students and faculty, is in the end, a counterproductive
> strategy for higher education. If the scholarly world is to
> maintain control of and access to its knowledge, both new
> and old, new cooperative ventures must be organized for the
> management of knowledge itself, rather than the ownership of
> formats (Battin, 1989).

Part of what keeps us focused on the smaller unit-of-analysis—the
campus—is the tendency of our institutions to use the size of the
campus library as a competitive factor. They fall into the trap of "bigger is better." As long as we continue to rank libraries on the basis of
the total number of holdings, we reinforce the suboptimization of
information resources. It is only when the available access to information is ubiquitous that we can gain the economies of scale and the
universal intellectual opportunities that are necessary. "Bigger is better" is not particularly meaningful in an electronic age, and is also an
entirely relative statement when the unit-of-analysis is that of a given
institution or set of institutions. We can no longer afford this competitive stance; it not only fails in terms of cost effectiveness, it is ultimately destructive.

The economic problems that have been ascribed to libraries in
this paper apply equally well to the basic structures of our educational
institutions. The old models are breaking down. Trying to "go it

alone," emphasizing independence over interdependence with our sister institutions, is not a principle that will succeed or endure much longer.

In his classic treatise on "The Idea of the University," the 19th century theologian John Henry Newman suggested that the library is the embalming of dead genius and that teaching was "the endowment of living [genius]" (Newman, 1976). In his reexamination of Newman's work, Jaroslav Pelikan emphasizes the interdependence of teaching and learning, and the essential role that libraries play in facilitating these educational functions:

> A university that would, in its enthusiasm for "living genius" or in its eagerness for "development" and "looking forward," neglect its vocation as a repository for "the oracles of the world's wisdom" and for the tradition would lose not only the past but the present and the future as well (Pelikan, 1992).

This living layer of teaching is built upon the top of past genius. In a coral reef, one finds a delicate, vital, living layer of coral polyps, grounded on the top of the calcium-based remnants of millions of previously living animals. To destroy or allow the erosion of the foundation of these stone-like structures will in turn cause the demise of the living reef. So, too, the destruction or erosion of our libraries has a vital relationship to teaching and learning, which in itself is the very basis of the vitality of society.

A reef also exemplifies the importance of looking at the right unit of analysis. When examining the ecosystem of the reef, it makes little sense to study a given cell, a particular coral polyp, or even a marvelous coral head. While each of these subunits may be of special interest, or particularly beautiful, none can survive in isolation if the ecosystem is under attack. It is the entire reef structure and ecosystem working together that provides the necessary structure, protection, nutrient base, and latticework that supports a much grander set of life forms. There is a richness of life on a coral reef, teeming with plant and animal life, all intermeshed with, supported by, and dependent on the dead remnants of centuries of previous generations of coral. These other animal and plant habitats are dependent on the coral structure of the past, and its destruction would result in the system collapse of many of these interdependent life forms.

If we look at the idea of the university, with its multiple functions, the "living genius" of teaching cannot live if we allow the "embalmed" genius of the library—this stone-like structure which reflects the accumulated information of the centuries—to be destroyed. Not only will the educational system be irreparably harmed, the impact on related systems and other dependent systems will also be felt, as Pelikan suggests when he states:

> The dynamic interrelation of research with teaching, and of both with the acquisition, preservation, and circulation of documents and artifacts, applies to galleries, museums, and above all to libraries (Pelikan, 1992).

As we enter an age of information, we must be vigilant in the preservation of the "embalmed genius" of the past in order to allow for the exciting "living genius" of teaching and research that are possible in a new electronic world. Preserving the "embalmed genius" is also essential if our society is to prevent the collapse of our system of higher education. Our success in saving the concept of the library will depend upon how quickly, thoroughly, and responsively we decide to react.

We must heed the warning signs and come up with new models for the 21st century, not try to sustain our old structures for their own sake. As Patricia Battin suggested several years ago:

> The persistent and futile attempt to finance contemporary information services from the conceptual and financial perspectives developed for a pretechnological age can only frustrate our aspirations and surely dilute the quality of research and instruction in our society (Battin, 1989).

The library of the future will be less a place where information is kept than a portal through which students and faculty will access the vast information resources of the world. This new library needs to bring together scholars and information resources without necessarily bringing either one to a physical building with a card catalog and books. The scholar may be at home or in her laboratory or in her classroom and the information may be in Kyoto or Bologna or on the surface of the moon. The library of the future will have the daunting task of helping scholars discover what relevant information exists, anywhere in the world and in a variety of formats and media.

The library of the future will be about access and knowledge-management, not about ownership. The hurdles that will be faced in creating this new electronic environment will most likely come from our unwillingness to break from our competitive tendencies, our parochialism in glorifying the past, and our unwillingness to accept the inevitability of change. Almost 150 years ago, Henry David Thoreau suggested that "Books are the treasured wealth of the world—the fit inheritance of generations and nations." It is yet to be determined whether our society is committed to making this inheritance a reality in the age of information.

REFERENCES

Battin, P. (1989). New ways of thinking about financing information services. In B. L. Hawkins (Ed.), *Organizing and Managing Information Resources on Campus.* EDUCOM.

Bush, V. (1945, July). As we may think. *Atlantic Monthly,* 176 (1), 101-108.

Cleveland, H. (1982, December 16). Information as a resource. *The Futurist,* 34-39.

Cleveland, H. (1985). *The knowledge executive: Leadership in an information society.* New York, NY: Truman Talley Books.

Cummings, A. M., White, M. L., Bowen, W. G., Lazarus, L. O., & Ekman, R. H. (1992). *University libraries and scholarly communication.* The Association of Research Libraries for the Andrew W. Mellon Foundation.

DeGennaro, R. (1990). Technology and access: The research library in transition. In *Organizing a research agenda: Information studies for the '90s.* Halifax, Nova Scotia.

Dougherty, R. M., & Hughes, C. (1991). *Preferred futures for libraries: A summary of six workshops with university provosts and library directors.* Mountain View, CA: The Research Libraries Group.

Getz, M. (1994). *Storing information in academic libraries.* Unpublished manuscript. Nashville, TN: Department of Economics and Business Administration, Vanderbilt University.

Gore, D. (1976). *Farewell to Alexandria: Solutions to space, growth, and performance problems of libraries.* Westport, CT: Greenwood Press.

Hawkins, B. L. (1994). Creating the library of the future: Incrementalism won't get us there! *The Serials Librarian,* 24 (3/4), 17-47.

Leighton, P. D., & Weber, D. C. (1986). *Planning academic and research library buildings.* Chicago, IL: American Library Association.

Matheson, N. W. (1988, May). Strategic management: Knowledge as a national resource. Paper presented at the Medical Librarians Association Annual Meeting, New Orleans, LA.

Newman, J. H. (1976). The idea of the university defined and illustrated I. In *Nine discourses delivered to the Catholics of Dublin II* (1852). In I. T. Ker (Ed.), *Occasional lectures and essays addressed to the members of the Catholic University* (1858). Oxford, England: Clarendon.

Okerson, A. (1992). The missing model: A 'Circle of Gifts.' *Serials Review,* 18 (1-2).

Pelikan, J. (1992). *The idea of the university: A reexamination.* New Haven, CT: Yale University Press.

Planning Task Force. (1996). *Building the national digital library: A federated approach.* National Digital Library Federation, Council of Library Resources.

Stubbs, K. L. (1992). *ARL statistics 1988-89 through 1990-91.* Association of Research Libraries. [http://arl.cni.org/stats/Statistics/stat.html]

Stubbs, K. L., & Molyneux, R. E. (1990). *Research library statistics 1907-08 through 1987-88.* Association of Research Libraries. [http://arl.cni.org/stats/Statistics/stat.html]

Suppes, P. (1966, September). The uses of computers in higher education. *Scientific American,* 214, 207.

University of Wisconsin faculty. (1996, May 6). University library committee report, faculty document 1214a. Madison, WI: University of Wisconsin.

Index

179